Project Portfolio Selection for Six Sigma

Also available from ASQ Quality Press:

The Executive Guide to Understanding and Implementing Lean Six Sigma
Robert M. Meisel, Steven J. Babb, Steven F. Marsh, and James P. Schlichting

Statistical Quality Control for the Six Sigma Green Belt
Bhisham C. Gupta and H. Fred Walker

The Certified Six Sigma Green Belt Handbook
Roderick A. Munro, Matthew J. Maio, Mohamed B. Nawaz, Govindarajan Ramu, and Daniel J. Zrymiak

Applying the Science of Six Sigma to the Art of Sales and Marketing
Michael J. Pestorius

Implementing Design for Six Sigma: A Leader's Guide
Georgette Belair and John O'Neill

Strategic Six Sigma for Champions: Keys to Sustainable Competitive Advantage
R. Eric Reidenbach and Reginald W. Goeke

Transactional Six Sigma for Green Belts: Maximizing Service and Manufacturing Processes
Samuel E. Windsor

Business Performance Through Lean Six Sigma: Linking the Knowledge Worker, the Twelve Pillars, and Baldrige
James T. Schutta

Six Sigma for the Next Millennium: A CSSBB Guidebook
Kim H. Pries

Lean Six Sigma for Healthcare: A Senior Leader Guide to Improving Cost and Throughput
Chip Caldwell, Jim Brexler, and Tom Gillem

Design for Six Sigma As Strategic Experimentation: Planning, Designing, and Building World-Class Products and Services
H. E. Cook

Computer-Based Robust Engineering: Essentials for DFSS
Genichi Taguchi, Rajesh Jugulum, and Shin Taguchi

To request a complimentary catalog of ASQ Quality Press publications, call 800-248-1946, or visit our Web site at http://qualitypress.asq.org.

Project Portfolio Selection for Six Sigma

William D. Mawby

ASQ Quality Press
Milwaukee, Wisconsin

American Society for Quality, Quality Press, Milwaukee 53203
© 2007 by ASQ
All rights reserved. Published 2007
Printed in the United States of America
13 12 11 10 09 08 07   5 4 3 2 1

Library of Congress Cataloging-in-Publication Data

Mawby, William D., 1952–
  Project portfolio selection for Six Sigma / William D. Mawby.
    p. cm.
  Includes bibliographical references and index.
  ISBN: 978-0-87389-707-5 (soft cover : alk. paper)
  1. Project management. 2. Six sigma (Quality control standard) 3. Total quality management. I. Title.

HD69.P75M3787 2007
658.4'013—dc22   2007009747

ISBN: 978-0-87389-707-5

No part of this book may be reproduced in any form or by any means, electronic, mechanical, photocopying, recording, or otherwise, without the prior written permission of the publisher.

Publisher: William A. Tony
Acquisitions Editor: Matt T. Meinholz
Project Editor: Paul O'Mara
Production Administrator: Randall Benson

ASQ Mission: The American Society for Quality advances individual, organizational, and community excellence worldwide through learning, quality improvement, and knowledge exchange.

Attention Bookstores, Wholesalers, Schools and Corporations: ASQ Quality Press books, videotapes, audiotapes, and software are available at quantity discounts with bulk purchases for business, educational, or instructional use. For information, please contact ASQ Quality Press at 800-248-1946, or write to ASQ Quality Press, P.O. Box 3005, Milwaukee, WI 53201-3005.

To place orders or to request a free copy of the ASQ Quality Press Publications Catalog, including ASQ membership information, call 800-248-1946. Visit our Web site at www.asq.org or http://qualitypress.asq.org.

Printed in the United States of America

 Printed on acid-free paper

Quality Press
600 N. Plankinton Avenue
Milwaukee, Wisconsin 53203
Call toll free 800-248-1946
Fax 414-272-1734
www.asq.org
http://www.asq.org/quality-press
http://standardsgroup.asq.org
E-mail: authors@asq.org

*I dedicate this work to my daughter Briana and wife LuAnne,
who make it all possible for me every day and in every way. If I shine
in any way it is only through the obscured reflection of their light.*

*I also dedicate this work to all the Six Sigma practitioners
who need some help in the area of project selection management.
I hope that this book will inspire you to look for fresh ideas from
the fertile operations research and financial engineering
arenas that will lead to deeper insights into your work.*

Table of Contents

Preface xi

Chapter 1   The Identification of Six Sigma Projects **1**
   The Promise of Six Sigma 1
   The Life Signs for Six Sigma 4
   The Emphasis on Six Sigma Projects 5
   The Essential Six Sigma Project 6

Chapter 2   Characteristics of Six Sigma Projects **9**
   Recommendations for Six Sigma Projects 9
   A Deeper Investigation into Recommended Project
      Characteristics 15
   The Advantages of Constructing a Portfolio 18
   Portfolios with Risk Constraints 21

Chapter 3   Multiple Criteria Decision Making Methods for
   Six Sigma Project Selection **25**
   The Need for Multiple Criteria 25
   Conversion of MCDM to a Common Criterion 26
   The Assigned-Weight MCDM Method 28
   Application of Assigned Weights to a Simple Problem .. 30
   Pareto-Optimal Approaches in MCDM 30
   Application of the Pareto MCDM Approach to a
      Complex Example 32
   Dominated Portfolios 32
   Recipes for the Methods Used in This Chapter 35

Chapter 4 The Analytic Hierarchy Approach to Project Portfolio Selection **37**
   The Problem with Assigned Weights 37
   The AHP Procedure 38
   A Simple AHP Application 39
   An AHP Example on Portfolios 42
   Problems with the AHP Approach 44
   Recipe for the Method Used in This Chapter............. 45

Chapter 5 The Data Envelopment Approach to Six Sigma Portfolio Selection **47**
   An Extension of the MCDM Pareto Method 47
   A Simple LP DEA Example............................. 49
   A Realistic DEA Application 55
   Extensions of the DEA Methods to Entire Portfolios 55
   Recipe for the Method Used in This Chapter............. 59

Chapter 6 Portfolio Selection Through Mathematical Programming **61**
   Constraints versus Objectives........................... 61
   Linear Programming Application to Six Sigma Project Portfolio Selection 63
   Sensitivity Analysis 71
   Recipe for the Method Used in This Chapter............. 73

Chapter 7 Six Sigma Project Portfolio Selection Through Integer Programming................................ **75**
   The Need for Integer Programming...................... 75
   A More Realistic Integer Programming Problem 79
   Adding More Constraints............................... 81
   Sensitivity Analysis for Integer Programming............. 85
   Recipe for the Method Used in This Chapter............. 91

Chapter 8 Measuring Portfolio Performance **93**
   What Is Portfolio Performance?......................... 93
   A Simple Approach 95
   Moving Toward Sensitivity.............................. 98
   Full Sensitivity-Based Performance Analysis 101
   Other Approaches..................................... 103

Chapter 9 Multiperiod and Multidivisional Approaches to Six Sigma Project Portfolio Selection **105**
   What Are Multiperiod and Multidivisional Problems? 105

A Multiperiod Example 106
A Multidivisional Example............................. 114
A Multidivisional and Multiperiod Problem 119

Chapter 10   Nonlinear Programming for Six Sigma Project Portfolio Selection **121**
The Need for Nonlinear Models........................ 121
A Simple Expository Example 123
Application of Nonlinear Programming to a Realistic Problem 124
The Addition of a Nonlinear Constraint................... 129
Nonlinear Sensitivity Analysis........................... 131
Recipe for the Method Used in This Chapter............... 133

Chapter 11   Options Pricing Approaches to Six Sigma Project Portfolio Selection **135**
The Need for Dynamic Allocation...................... 135
What Options Are..................................... 136
A Simple Options Pricing Approach to Project Selection 137
Options Pricing Approach Applied to a Realistic Portfolio Problem 140
Options Pricing with Different Transition Probabilities 144
Options on Project Portfolios........................... 147
Decision Analysis and Simulation Methods................ 147
Risk Mitigation Approaches............................. 148
Recipe for the Method Used in This Chapter............... 149

Chapter 12   Summary and Outlook for Six Sigma Project Portfolio Selection **151**
Six Sigma and Project Selection........................ 151
Ranking Methods and Multiple Objectives 152
Linear and Integer Programming Methods 153
Nonlinear Programming and Options Methods.............. 154
Some Guidelines for the Use of the Methods............... 155
The Future of Six Sigma Project Portfolio Selection 158

Bibliography *161*
Index.. *163*

Preface

Six Sigma is one of the most popular and successful process improvement programs that has ever existed. It achieves this level of success through a combination of statistical methods, an emphasis on bottom-line results, and a strict project management approach. The majority of Six Sigma publications and presentations seem to deal with either the administration of projects, the area of application of the methods, or the details of the utilization of the statistical methods. These are undeniably important topics and it is good that they seem to be adequately covered by available materials. However, there is one area that seems to be given mostly lip-service in the Six Sigma literature and yet at the same time is considered critical to the success of the whole improvement endeavor. This is the topic of Six Sigma project selection.

Most Six Sigma project selection methods seem to assume that each individual project should be selected on its own merit, without much regard to other funded projects. While this approach of ranking each project separately can lead to reasonable performance of the whole portfolio of Six Sigma projects, it exposes management to a larger than necessary risk. This book shows in detail how the current methods can be improved through the application of well-developed methods from operations research and financial engineering, which treat the project selection problem from the viewpoint of portfolio selection. These techniques range from fairly straightforward extensions of the ranking methods by multicriteria methods to sophisticated mathematical programming methods that allow one to select portfolios with exquisite control and specificity. All of the methods will, in general, produce Six Sigma project portfolios that outperform their counterparts selected through non-portfolio type methods. Sometimes this advantage can be quite substantial depending on the variety of projects and the level of constraints that operate during the selection process.

Although it can be argued that Six Sigma is successful without these methods, it can also be argued that no program, of any name, can depend on continued support from an organization unless it uses its allocated resources in the most efficient manner possible. As companies become more mature in their Six Sigma programs it is almost a certainty that companies will demand more benefits using fewer resources, and with verification that their methods are financially sound. There is also an argument that true believers in Six Sigma should look for improvements in all areas, including their own programs, and specifically in their less-than-optimal project selection methods. The author of this book would also pose one other argument: that Six Sigma practitioners should read, understand, and apply the methods presented in this book. And that is because they are methods that are standard in other fields, specifically operations research and financial engineering, that appear to have much potential benefit for Six Sigma but which are more or less ignored by practitioners. Such a "closed shop" seems to be a dangerous approach and this author hopes that this book can lead to some inroads in this area.

Finally, a word of two should be written about the approach taken in this book to emphasize the financial payback of Six Sigma project portfolio selection. This is a purposeful bias that the author feels is critical for the future of Six Sigma. The only feature of Six Sigma programs that seems to distinguish them from the myriad of other improvement approaches that have appeared and disappeared over the last 20 years is this strict requirement of verifiable financial impact. And yet, at least to the author, this feature is receiving less and less emphasis in modern discussion of the approach, and the author fears that if this trend continues, it is quite possible that Six Sigma will lose support and fall by the wayside. If anyone thinks this is impossible, please talk to any veteran practitioner of SPC or TQM and one may get a different opinion. There is little doubt today that business needs what Six Sigma has to offer, and good managers will continue to demand more and more accountability in the use of limited resource monies to generate benefits. This book is an attempt to put Six Sigma project selection methods on a sound financial basis so they will continue to be the 'go-to' approach far into the future.

1

The Identification of Six Sigma Projects

THE PROMISE OF SIX SIGMA

Six Sigma is one of the most successful process improvement endeavors ever implemented. The seminal attempt to employ Six Sigma was a program initiated at Motorola in 1986. This Six Sigma program was the culmination of a series of statistical quality improvement activities that were tried at the company as, at least in part, a response to the pressure brought on U.S. companies by the successful application of Deming's methodologies in Japan. By most accounts this initial effort was successful, but due to the subsequent massive implementation of Six Sigma at General Electric in the 1990s, history has assigned to it the role of precursor. Under the aggressive leadership of GE's management and the tremendous technical expertise of their support scientists, this program has taken on near-legendary proportions. Statements of costs of this effort were quoted in the millions of U.S. dollars while claims of annual gains reached into the billions of U.S. dollars! As difficult as it is sometimes to separate the facts from the hype, it seems clear that there is something special about the Six Sigma approach to process improvement. Figure 1.1 shows a sampling of the claims made in regard to the General Electric Six Sigma program (Harry 2006).

It did not take long for quality-hungry colleagues and competitors to pick up on the success of the Six Sigma approach and make an attempt to adapt it for their own organizations. As a result of this surge of interest there appeared Six Sigma conferences, papers, books, and training courses that each offered their own view of the details of its implementation. Consultants who were already engaged in the previous quality and process

2   Chapter One

- Tenfold increase in CT scanner and x-ray tube production
- $400 million investment dollars saved in plastics
- 80,000 employees trained in Six Sigma
- $17 billion in cash generated in slow economy
- More than 500,000 projects completed
- Six Sigma appears more than 64 times in annual report

Figure 1.1   A sampling of claims about Six Sigma success at GE.

- Air Academy Associates
- Celerant Institute
- Extreme Quality Mexico
- Global Consultants Inc.
- MKC Six Sigma
- Process Solutions International
- Quality Inspection and Training Services
- Six Sigma Canada
- Targettech (Shanghai) Ltd.
- Venturehaus
- Young Associates Ltd.

Figure 1.2   Some Six Sigma support companies.

improvement approaches quickly retooled or at least relabeled their wares and before long an entire cottage industry grew up to support the needs of companies trying to emulate GE's success. Since much of the technical tool set of Six Sigma is identical to that of older statistical process control and statistical quality assurance approaches, it was relatively easy to reinvigorate old programs by associating them with Six Sigma. Today it is hard to find an organization that provides or supports process improvement that does not associate itself with Six Sigma in some fashion. Figure 1.2 lists just a few organizations that offer support for Six Sigma from the 12 pages of hits generated by a casual Internet search (Six Sigma 2006).

Such excitement and energy cannot help but stimulate the development of new programs that either tweak the fundamental Six Sigma process or attempt to expand it into new and interesting hybrids. One of the most successful of these hybrids seems to be the combination of Six Sigma with lean manufacturing in an approach usually called Lean Six Sigma (George 2000). Lean manufacturing concentrates on methods that can be used to reduce wasted process time and enhance just-in-time manufacturing. Other developments stress the application of Six Sigma to nonmanufacturing processes such as those employed in accounting, administration, and research departments. More recently the medical field has become an important focus for these programs. Other practitioners have put their emphasis on the *design for Six Sigma* aspect of the approach and made this activity a cornerstone of some of the more recent developments in the field. Figure 1.3 lists some of the Six Sigma application areas and spin-offs that are being marketed today (Wikipedia 2006).

The application of Six Sigma concepts and tools to the management of general decision processes (Mawby 2005) is one of the more recent spin-offs from the main body of activity in this area.

Any methodology that grows so fast and sprouts so many viable offshoots is bound to mutate, evolve, and be reinterpreted by just about every new person who catches hold of it. In the case of Six Sigma there are so many adaptations and reformulations of the basic approach that it is difficult, if not impossible, to pin down the precise definition of a Six Sigma program. One can find nearly as many different interpretations and commentaries on the program as one has patience to research. Some interpretations emphasize that Six Sigma is best seen as a culture of perfectionism that uses a disciplined methodology to move processes nearer to perfection. Other references describe in great detail how the creation of Yellow, Green, Black, and Master Black Belts is the critical component of a system that rewards success, promotes the successful, and intimately integrates the system into the business reality. Still other experts stress the define–measure–analyze–improve–control, or DMAIC, cycle that enables project teams to focus on a sequence of solid tactical steps that can dramatically improve their chance of success.

- Design for Six Sigma
- Six Sigma for medical processes
- Six Sigma for administrative processes
- Six Sigma for information technologies
- Six Sigma for education
- Six Sigma for information quality
- Six Sigma for decision quality

Figure 1.3 Extended Six Sigma application areas.

THE LIFE SIGNS FOR SIX SIGMA

It is therefore not a simple task to distill from this complicated mixture the few active ingredients of a successful Six Sigma program. But there are clearly some elements that are common to most of the approaches and these are listed in Figure 1.4. A closer look at each of these elements will demonstrate that each seems to be a curious but practical mixture of old and new wisdom, and they make it clear that a program based on these elements would likely be something unique among improvement approaches.

At first it seems somewhat strange that Six Sigma programs should place so much weight on implementation through a measured sequence of structured projects. After all, there are many companies that have found great success with employee suggestions and work teams. The ideas generated in this fashion by operators and line supervisors are likely to be simplistic but they can usually be implemented efficiently, inexpensively, and they can lead to near-perfection of a process. On the other hand, such a gradual approach is unlikely to lead to any dramatic process breakthroughs. The very proximity of the employees to their processes can lead to tunnel vision that keeps them from finding the big improvements. Alternatively, the Six Sigma approach tends to deliberately choose challenging tasks that will lead to breakthroughs once they are completed. In some sense this approach might better be labeled as statistical process innovation rather than statistical process improvement. Six Sigma is probably best suited to companies who have already done the work to make their processes mature and who now need to make more dramatic leaps in performance. This need for salutary improvements seems to provide the rationale to support the fact that Six Sigma depends on a series of structured projects, which will become the primary focus of most of the later chapters in this book.

The second common element of a successful Six Sigma program is its stressing that process improvement expenditures and gains must be placed on an equal financial basis with other efforts like capacity increases, machinery upgrades, and management initiatives. There is an insistence that projects must be held accountable for showing positive measurable impacts on the firm's bottom line. This is an important and significant departure

- Structured series of projects
- Must be connected to bottom-line results
- Employees well trained in statistics and motivated to employ them

Figure 1.4 Some common elements of Six Sigma programs.

from the way in which improvement programs were often managed before the advent of Six Sigma, where such investments were often pursued simply because it seemed to be the right thing to do or to please an auditor. Many veterans of withered process improvement programs think that it is primarily this lack of a direct connection to company finances that hurt their efforts over the long haul. Most programs can survive for a short while based just on management hope, but it seems clear that programs must somehow become profit centers for the company if they are to continue to get adequate funding indefinitely. It is much to the credit of the Six Sigma approach that it meets head-on this challenge of making the improvement activity an equal partner with other business concerns. This deep and intimate connection of Six Sigma results with financial gain is one the motivations for the approach taken in this book.

The final element common to many Six Sigma programs is that they recognize the need to have as many employees as possible use statistical methods correctly and efficiently. Even today it is not common for most employees to enter into their positions with adequate training and so it is left to a program like Six Sigma to make up for the deficiency. This implies that there must be a well-developed training regimen that is readily available to all appropriate employees. Any attempt to teach material as sophisticated as modern statistical methods demands that there be at least three organizational features present in the organization. Firstly, there must be a source of professional statistical advice to choose and ground these methods. This expertise is often best provided by a set of corporate-level degreed statisticians who are well grounded in shop floor applications. Secondly, there must be well-documented, readily available training that is tied to statistical software. This training should be as standardized as possible and should be required of an employee for significant professional development. Thirdly, students have to have the proper motivation to make the learning successful. There must be some kind of systematic reward or encouragement to provide this motivation, and it must be clear to all the employees that hard work in this arena will lead to benefits for them. It is also important to include all levels of management in Six Sigma Champion training so they can support and demand proper application of the methods by those they supervise.

THE EMPHASIS ON SIX SIGMA PROJECTS

Although all three elements listed in Figure 1.4 are considered to be essential to the success of a Six Sigma program, it is the critical element of structured projects that will be the focus of this work. It seems especially important to focus on this aspect both because it is essential and because it is somewhat neglected in the literature. For example, the statistical tool set for Six Sigma has been the subject of many books and training regimens. There seems to be no need to provide any further discussion on this topic in this book. Likewise there is extensive material readily available on the design and construction of training programs for Six Sigma practitioners and program Champions. In addition, there is plenty of good software accompanied by excellent manuals and training programs that need no additional coverage here (Brassard 2001).

On the other hand, there is little material that trains one in the details of the process of making the Six Sigma projects an integral part of the bottom line of a company. This could become a weak point in many fledgling improvement programs. The specific details of the project accounting system are, of course, dependent on the particular company and it would be quite difficult to cover them in any useful way in this book. A more fruitful approach is to demonstrate a variety of possible approaches that can then be adapted by the reader to whatever system she is constrained to use. This book has the goal of providing this demonstration with enough accompanying details to support implementation. Beyond this immediate objective, there is a secondary objective to pry open a bit the somewhat closed door that many a Six Sigma program has erected against ideas that have been developed in other fields. Many of the methodologies in this book come directly from two fields that have been neglected in this way: financial management and operations research. It is the hope of the author that if the reader finds value in the tools presented here that they will go on to explore more fully these other fields. Doing so would likely bring immediate and substantial benefits for current Six Sigma programs and might just keep them vital into future decades.

THE ESSENTIAL SIX SIGMA PROJECT

A project is a set of activities that consumes resources and produces measurable results in a well-defined time period (Westcott 2004). Projects are defined by their objectives, their resources, and their timelines. They succeed or fail on the strengths of their project teams and the will of their support organizations to pursue them. It is probably fair to say that most quality and productivity professionals, that is, the likely project leaders and team members, think of projects as activities and not as investments. In their minds they probably tend to emphasize the potential of the improvement and the technical difficulties associated with achieving it over the actual financial payback that is achieved. Managers, on the other hand, have the job of seeing the projects as investments that tie up limited resources and, hopefully, yield gains and benefits. They tend to focus on the constraints of money, time, and resources rather than on the sheer technical potential. Both viewpoints are, of course, valid, but in this book the primary viewpoint will be to treat the project as an investment. The methods presented here will not deal specifically with project management or with team development but will concentrate on the proper selection of projects in order to produce financial benefits. Viewed in this way as an investment, the Six Sigma project must be evaluated financially as well as technically. Once this financial aspect is accepted it becomes easy to demonstrate that the best way in which to select Six Sigma projects is to consider them as an integral part of a coordinated portfolio of such projects.

In most of the more progressive companies, project selection is done in support of a business plan. Such a business plan should try to assess customer needs, translate them into doable internal activities, and then allocate resources to their execution. Often the business plan is coordinated across company entities and also through several planning periods so it can be quite complex and constrained. But once the general targets are set, the selection of actual projects is often done in a less integrated manner. Specifically, in companies in which Six Sigma projects provide the fundamental motor for driving these projects, it is common to view the projects as separate, independent activities that need have only minimal cross-coordination. In those cases in which project coordination is attempted, it tends to be rather subjective and can fail to be as effective as it could be. This is not to indict the current methods, since it can be argued that they have been effective most of the time, but this book contends that it could be dangerous to continue with this approach as companies demand more and more justification for expenditures. And this suboptimality can be quite severe for companies that have minimal or inadequate Six Sigma resources. The methods presented in this book can be used to improve the project selection process in a way that should make it much easier to secure proper funding levels. One can get wildly better performance from a well-coordinated portfolio of projects than from the typical disjointed collection. This improvement in performance can be as much as 50 percent in realistic situations and could very well spell the difference between the death and the success of a Six Sigma program.

Few experts in this area doubt that there is great importance in choosing the set of Six Sigma projects wisely but even fewer go on to discuss any of the methods for effective project selection that are presented here. And, yet, these methods are well documented and have proven successful in multiple, diverse fields of application over many years of use. Chapter 2 will set the stage for introducing these more effective methods by providing an extensive description of the typical Six Sigma project selection method. It will be seen that this method can perform adequately if one's focus is solely on project execution but that it can be improved upon and that the level of this improvement can grow quite dramatically as the numbers of constraints and considerations increases. Further chapters will then introduce and demonstrate a wide variety of improved techniques, including approaches to balance multiple objectives, determine efficient horizons, and choose optimal portfolios through linear and integer programming.

2
Characteristics of Six Sigma Projects

RECOMMENDATIONS FOR SIX SIGMA PROJECTS

Six Sigma (George 2000) is formulated on the dynamic of making continual improvements in processes through a structured system of projects. These projects are to be conducted by personnel who are well trained in powerful statistical methods and are supported by management committed to the program. Furthermore, these projects should have objectives that produce verifiable gains that are directly integrated into the overall company improvement plan. An improvement plan is a multiyear strategy that seeks aggressive enhancements across all processes of an organization including research, manufacturing, and administration. The define–measure–analyze–improve–control (DMAIC) cycle often serves as a guide for the sequence of steps that are pursued in each project. The DMAIC cycle is a commonsense algorithm for implementing the scientific approach to problem solving coupled with follow-up to make the gains stick. There is overwhelming evidence that a serious application of the Six Sigma approach can produce valuable results. See Figure 2.1 for an illustration of the process.

But is this process as good as it could be? The philosophy of Six Sigma clearly considers all processes, including the Six Sigma process itself, to be capable of improvement. Thus there is an assumption that some sort of meta-level application of the Six Sigma approach to studying its own processes should be done. And one of the subprocesses that is likely to be most affected by this self-study is the process of project selection.

10 Chapter Two

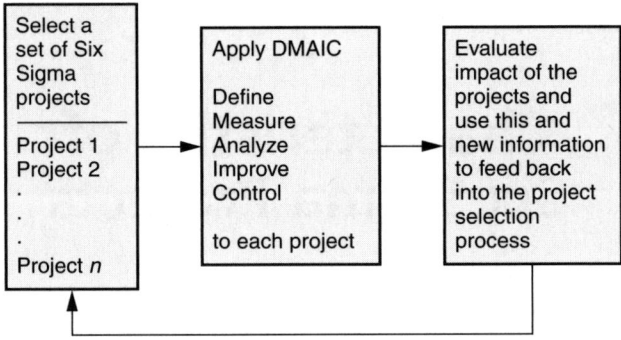

Figure 2.1 Six Sigma uses the DMAIC approach implemented through projects.

To understand this potential benefit more fully it is necessary to investigate the usual methods of project selection that are often employed in current Six Sigma programs. Many Six Sigma references (Brassard and Ritter 2001) and experts recommend a ranking approach to project selection. Fundamentally, this process has four steps. The first step is the pronouncement by upper management of general areas for improvement that are likely to be strategic for the company. One such area for improvement might, for example, be the objective of reducing customer complaints associated with the newly released product model by 10 percent before the end of the current calendar year. Such business directives should ideally be part of an overall improvement plan that sets objectives from a multiyear and multidivisional perspective. Clearly, a sensible improvement plan must be calibrated with customer needs through some kind of *voice of the customer* (VOC) process. Depending of the size of the Six Sigma company and the importance of the customer, these needs might translate into mandatory projects. But usually these needs are translated indirectly through the agency of company management and there is considerable leeway in selecting which projects can best support them. Six Sigma emphasizes that however these directives are expressed, they should be translated into project outputs that are measurable and financially beneficial.

The second step is that specific project proposals should be generated to match these business improvement directives. These ideas might be generated by management, by engineers, by technicians, or from operators. Because Six Sigma is usually not implemented as an outgrowth of an employee suggestion program, it is more likely that projects are chosen by managerial and technical staff, but no good idea should ever be ignored. Depending on the company process, these proposals might have widely varying levels of detail but they must contain a fairly complete description of the project in terms of potential gain, costs, necessary resources, and required support requirements in order to be considered as viable candidates for funding. In almost every practical situation there tends to be many more proposed projects than can ever be reasonably funded, so it is important that projects be fleshed out enough to allow the selection committee to make intelligent judgments about their merits. Usually, the members of this selection committee are managers who, while familiar to some extent with the project details, are not technical experts on all of them. To ensure that projects are described in enough detail to enable this selection committee to make reasonable decisions about funding, there are usually some basic rules that determine the types of information that must be available for each project. In the majority of cases this means that there is a set of standard characteristics for each project that are defined according to the internal requirements of the company in terms of asset management, cost accounting, and investment protocol. For the purpose of this book, it will be assumed at the very least that this set of characteristics contains information on the gain and the cost of each project. In addition, it is assumed that there are always additional variable characteristics on project risk, business objectives, customer requirements, and training needs that must be considered as well but that will be specific to the projects themselves or the company considering them.

The third step concerns the submission of these project proposals to the review and selection committee. This review might be quite formal, with various prescribed steps and even a formal presentation of the project details, but most Six Sigma references suggest that the ideal project selection process is essentially a ranking procedure. Due to the fact that there are too many projects, there may first be a preliminary screening step that removes some projects by comparing their characteristics to a set of requirements on cost to benefit ratio, or payback period, or some other criterion. Alternately, these same criteria can be used to separate the potential projects into budgeting categories such as those that respond to customer requests, those that are for cost reduction, and those that are strategic in nature. If the company chooses to fund these different kinds of projects from different budget buckets, then subsequent project ranking and selection activities usually take place within each separate category.

At the fourth step, the possibly reduced set of proposed projects is then reviewed and a subset of them is chosen for funding. In many companies this review process takes place in an all-day forum in which politics and subjectivity can be the dominant influences and the final project list is more a reflection of managerial personalities than any attempt at creating a scientifically organized portfolio. It is clear that some subjective input can be important since it is impossible to capture all pertinent details in a limited set of characteristics, but too much subjectivity can lead quickly to suboptimal decisions.

More structured companies have preset, established methods that can at least provide a preliminary ranking of the potential projects. These Six Sigma project ranking methods are described in greater detail below. But even without full disclosure of these methods, it is easy to see that it can be difficult for a committee of peer managers, each with his or her own personal agenda, to choose a properly integrated set of projects to fund. This inability to produce an efficient or optimal portfolio of projects is likely to be a weakness of these ranking methods. To comprehend how such a choice of good projects can lead to a poorly performing portfolio it is perhaps instructive to think in terms of sports teams, where a poorly coordinated all-star team can be outperformed by a well-balanced set of more ordinary players. Or one can think of financial portfolios that mitigate risk by carefully balancing the types of investments. It is this coordination of objectives that even the best project-by-project ranking methods can miss. The Six Sigma project selection and execution process is illustrated in Figure 2.2.

Along with the four mandatory requirements listed above for the selection and management of Six Sigma projects, there are three other considerations that can also have a major influence on the success of the projects selection process in specific situations. One of these considerations concerns the fact that investment plans are not entirely static. Most such plans tend to change throughout the fiscal year due to unexpected shortfalls or unanticipated developments with the projects themselves. Therefore it can be important to have some accepted mechanism by which project decisions may be reviewed and, if necessary, funds reallocated. For example, a failing but critical project may be reengineered at the expense of other ongoing or planned activities. Or a project may discover that its potential gain has grown fivefold and yet its original ranking leaves it without sufficient

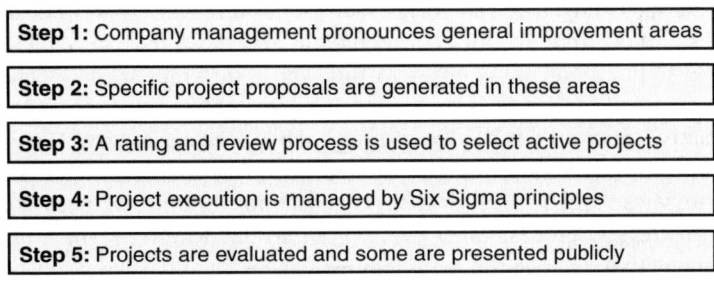

Figure 2.2 The Six Sigma project selection and execution process.

Characteristics of Six Sigma Projects 13

resources to realize the gain in a timely fashion. On the other hand, it can be unwise to alter the plans too quickly. This not only can jeopardize the success of the projects but often increases their indirect and direct costs. Most Six Sigma programs depend on the project leader to judge when such changes are necessary and to bring them to the attention of management at periodically scheduled review sessions that are held perhaps four times a year. In a similar vein there must also be a sensible mechanism for deciding whether a particular project should be funded at all. Often there is a ceiling set on the money to be spent in a calendar year on improvement projects. The ranking process may allocate most of these funds to one big project, squeezing out a number of smaller projects that could provide great value if they were viewed cumulatively. Under some scenarios it might be better to add a little more money to the pot or to not use all the money allocated. Lastly, there must be some sort of evaluation process in which the expected performance of the project is compared to its actual performance. Most Six Sigma programs simply count the gains made without evaluating the other characteristics that were provided for the project. However, it is important to check on risk analyses and on estimates of timing, and so on, both to determine the real value of the particular process at hand and also to provide an analysis to serve as the basis for further improvement of the process. Figure 2.3 summarizes these other concerns.

From many Six Sigma reference books one gets the idea that projects are chosen mainly to provide chances to evaluate the performance of employees. In these references it is recommended that projects be chosen so that they are appropriately challenging for the level of the Belt who is involved with them. They must be easy enough for Green Belts, right-sized for Black Belts, and challenging enough for Master Black Belts. If the purpose of the Six Sigma program is simply to build a bigger program with more trained employees and more belted individuals, then this sort of approach makes sense. In this case, one would be tempted to do many small easy projects that produce no measurable gains but produce lots of training and belt attainment opportunities. When training opportunities are not the sole objective, then there is nearly always some target set on project benefit. Sometimes this is pure monetary gain, or it can be return on investment,

---

1. Must have some mechanism for updating projects funding
2. Must have some mechanism for deciding between current and delayed funding
3. Must have some informed method for evaluating performance

Figure 2.3 Secondary concerns in Six Sigma project selection.

or perhaps even a properly chosen utility function. Sometimes this kind of requirement is merely applied as a filter to sort out projects by which color belt the leader should have. If one takes a more financial approach to these gains, then one might be tempted to maximize these gains rather than have them entered as a constraint. This focus on financial optimization is a critical feature of the project portfolio. Regardless of the exact handling of gains it can be generally conceded that most Six Sigma programs will not survive if they do not provide substantial positive impact on the company's bottom line.

Although the ranking can vary greatly from one Six Sigma implementation to another, it is possible to gain a sense of the type of characteristics that are usually considered for each project (Brassard and Ritter 2001), which are summarized in Figure 2.4.

Once a project achieves these requirements it is then given a charter, assigned a leader, and proceeds into project execution phase. It is only at this point that suitable process indicators can be chosen. Examples of good process indicators include those on the list presented in Figure 2.5.

- The project must align with key business objectives
- The project must have strong financial benefit
- The project scope should be at the plant/divisional level
- The project difficulty should be more than daily activity
- The project should have adequate historical data
- The project should focus on a preexisting process
- The project should be well supported

Figure 2.4 The recommended characteristics for a Six Sigma project.

- Nonconformance rates
- Error rates
- Average level of a quantity
- Standard deviation of a quantity
- Time of delivery
- Reliability of a system
- Satisfaction index rating

Figure 2.5 Some good process indicators.

These indicators are meant to help the project team have something concrete to track in the work that is easier to manage than monetary gains. Despite the obvious practicality of these process indicators, note well that Six Sigma program projects must move beyond indicators and produce monetary gains if they are to grow and prosper. This is similar to the situation in which one can invest based on Dow Jones averages or inflation levels but it is the actual monetary gains that can result from these decisions that are ultimately most important.

A DEEPER INVESTIGATION INTO RECOMMENDED PROJECT CHARACTERISTICS

It is now possible to take a closer look at the Six Sigma project characteristics that are the primary features on which selection procedure can operate. The first one, dealing with the alignment of the project with an appropriate business strategy, is often difficult to evaluate. The motivation behind this characteristic is that each project should have a direct positive impact on one or more key performance indicators. In most cases, unless there is an overriding requirement from customers or business needs, this can depend on what is primarily a judgment call. Many of the activities will be either naturally related to one of the broad categories for improvement that are set by upper management or can be recast in ways to make them seem as if they are. This is just part of company politics and most employees will know how to play this game from long years of practice. Some of the arbitrariness of this approach can be reduced by introducing a scale for this characteristic that assigns a number from one to six based on the degree of its relatedness to business objectives. But who should assign this rating? From a purely practical perspective, this characteristic usually does no more than ensure that one or more of the key process indicators are at least mentioned in the project description.

The second characteristic is that the project should have a strong financial impact. Now this seems to be a more solidly measurable characteristic and, as such, is one of the primary sources of inspiration for this book. But even in this case there must be some choices made. There will be expenses for the project. Should these be subtracted from the actual gains? If the improvement achieves a gain that is not punctual but has a continuing payback, then it is critical to select a definite time horizon over which to compute the gain. And what about the time value of money? Should one use some kind of discounting in the calculation of monetary gain? Maybe one should compute a real options value or an opportunity loss–based value. Whatever the final definition of monetary gain, Six Sigma programs depend on achieving large monetary gains so this characteristic must be carefully crafted.

The third characteristic is that of requiring that the scope of the proposed project be at the plant or divisional level. The rationale for this characteristic is to provide a guarantee that the project has large monetary values, has high visibility across the company, and probably is of medium to high risk. One could argue that there are more direct characteristics that meet the same needs, such as direct measures of monetary gain, project risk, and organizational balance.

The fourth characteristic is that the project addresses a problem that is not solved or considered not solvable with normal improvement methods. This seems to be a reasonable objective but does it add much information? If the intention is to choose activities that require special effort and teamwork to achieve, then this could be mixed up with the very definition of a project. And how is this decided? It would appear to require a team to even assess the difficulty of the project. Or perhaps the key is to distinguish those tasks that require full project resources from those that do not need them. This all indicates that this characteristic is targeted at providing adequate training and leadership experiences and it might be better accomplished by directly measuring these impacts.

The fifth characteristic, that the project has adequate supporting data, seems to be primarily aimed at evaluating risk. A project without supporting data will almost always take longer than one that has such data. So the cost will certainly increase relative to this delay, but it is the risk that often goes up most substantially. Longer projects with IS requirements may require data collection schemes, data storage, and data cleansing. Because of lack of data, the validity of any proposed technical solution is more tentative as well. But why not directly establish some risk measures and use them? This will be the approach of the portfolio selection process that is described below.

A sixth characteristic is that the improvement be based on a preexisting process rather than on the development of a completely novel one. This seems to be related again to risk and cost containment. In almost all cases, the creation of a new process is more risky than planning an improvement of an old one. On the other hand, an approach that is constrained to fit into existing processes will probably limit the potential gains as well. It seems more likely that improvements would be incremental under this method rather than breakthroughs. An approach that considers the project risk more directly would seem to be a valid alternative approach for these purposes.

The seventh characteristic is that the project should have solid support from team members and supporting personnel. Clearly this again has a lot to do with cost and risk containment. A well-supported project would seem to be less difficult to achieve and therefore would seem to have lower risk of failure. But there are difficulties in measuring this characteristic. It is quite common to get nominal support for a project in the selection committee only to have resources withheld or withdrawn when they are actually needed. The intention of this characteristic is sensible but seems again to be too indirect. A more direct, well-defined risk would make the projects selection process more visible and straightforward. These characteristics of good Six Sigma projects are summarized in Figure 2.4, page 14.

It therefore seems reasonable to reinterpret this set of recommendations for selecting Six Sigma projects as primarily an attempt to ensure good monetary gain at some preestablished level of risk. Cost of the projects is also involved in a critical way but mostly as an overall budget constraint on the number and size of projects that can be undertaken at any one time. There certainly can be secondary characteristics such as training opportunities and degree of alignment of the projects with business objectives that can be considered in the selection process but they are clearly not dominant. These fundamental characteristics of gain, cost, and risk are also commonly used in the management of financial investments. There may be different measures of performance in the financial arena like stock prices, volatilities, and capital asset performance measures (CAPM), but it is clear that this field shares many features with the Six Sigma project selection process (SAS Institute 1994). And just as a common solution to the financial challenge is a properly chosen portfolio of instruments, so it will be demonstrated that a well-chosen portfolio of projects can bring substantial benefits to Six Sigma project selection as well.

It is also important to note that the usual recommendations for project characteristics that have been discussed seem to view gain as the primordial objective, with cost, risk, and other secondary characteristics as constraints or secondary objectives. Although the practical application of Six Sigma may not always adhere strictly to this viewpoint, this book will assume that such an approach is always the ultimate target. It is easy to justify this assumption by considering each characteristic and evaluating whether there is likely to be an upper (or lower) limit on its values that is important to the project selection committee. It is hard to believe that anyone would put a limit on gain as long as it exceeded cost. However, it is almost certain that there would be an upper limit on project cost and allowable risk. In the same way, there would likely be lower limits on secondary characteristics like the number of Black Belt projects or the number of business

18 Chapter Two

> Objective is to maximize the financial gain achieved from the project
>
> Constraint of minimum gain
> Constraint of minimum risk due to project scope
> Constraint of minimum risk due to data inadequacy
> Constraint of minimum risk due to choosing a new process
> Constraint of minimum risk due to lack of support for the project
> Constraint of total allowable budget
> Constraint of available resources

Figure 2.6 The features of the financial approach to projects.

objectives that are treated by the portfolio. This understanding only reinforces the connection between the portfolio approach to Six Sigma project selection and financial portfolio management. Figure 2.6 lists some financial features of projects.

THE ADVANTAGES OF CONSTRUCTING A PORTFOLIO

If there were only a single proposed project then there would be no difficulty in the selection process and all the challenge would be in the execution. Even a set of projects would pose no problem if there were no limits on the total money available or on the allowable risk. The existence of constraints is what makes it difficult to choose the best set of projects from the full set of potential ones. And the more constraints one adds to the mix, the more difficult it will be, in general, to find the best portfolio. The details of the methods for constructing better portfolios will be given in later chapters, but for now one of these methods will be used here without explanation as a concrete demonstration of the potential differences between the typical ranking methods and the better portfolio approach.

Consider an example in which there are 20 possible projects. For each project there is a set of standardized characteristics that includes anticipated gains in thousands of dollars per annum, an expected total cost of the project, and an estimate of the risk associated with the project. This risk gives the likelihood as assessed by the project authors that the project gain and cost will be achieved exactly as they are captured in the proposal. This risk is due to the many technical or administrative difficulties that can arise during the implementation of the project. The example list is shown in Table 2.1.

Consider three methods of assignment for this portfolio. For the first method, consider a random selection of projects that is continued until the total budget limit is reached. No organization is likely to survive for long based on such a random selection of projects, but it is important to have a baseline against which to compare the different methods. In the financial world from which many of the tools presented in this book are borrowed it is common to use a random selection of stocks as a baseline for evaluating portfolio performance. It is in this same sense of constructing a baseline that the random project selection is made. It is definitely not considered to be a viable project selection mechanism for use in Six Sigma. Any procedure that does not substantially outperform a random choice of projects should clearly be considered as totally inadequate.

For the second method, consider a ranking method that would be much more commonly used in real businesses and is often the only method used in

Table 2.1 A realistic set of potential Six Sigma project characteristics.

Project number	Gain in K$	Cost in K$	Percent risk
Project 1	94	20	15
Project 2	182	95	7
Project 3	76	66	24
Project 4	76	64	2
Project 5	68	12	7
Project 6	518	31	42
Project 7	176	6	14
Project 8	746	9	15
Project 9	372	26	10
Project 10	1048	24	44
Project 11	254	47	40
Project 12	184	11	14
Project 13	178	14	44
Project 14	1622	13	31
Project 15	1144	75	8
Project 16	120	29	40
Project 17	230	26	40
Project 18	494	30	36
Project 19	174	28	11
Project 20	610	10	46

Six Sigma project selection. This method depends on a strict ranking of the potential projects by monetary gain. Given this ranked order, it is assumed that the projects are funded until the overall budget cap is reached.

As the last Six Sigma project selection method, consider the integer programming method that will described in all its technical detail in Chapter 7. This method is mathematically guaranteed to give the project portfolio with the highest gain that still satisfies all the given constraints. This portfolio cannot be out-achieved if the assumptions used to construct the solution are valid and all the important constraints are included. So the purpose of the demonstration is not simply to show that the portfolio method outperforms the ranking methods, for this is mathematically guaranteed, but rather it is to illustrate the size of the potential differences between the three methods.

The randomly chosen portfolio consists of projects 20, 2, 19, 1, 12, and 7. The estimated gain from this portfolio is computed by adding the individual gains

$$= \$610K + \$182K + \$174K + \$94K + \$184K + \$176K = \$1420K.$$

The cost of this random portfolio is the sum of all the individual costs

$$= \$10K + \$95K + \$28K + \$20K + \$11K + \$6K = \$170K$$

out of the possible $200K that is available. Clearly many other portfolios could be randomly chosen. Some could do better than this one and others would likely do worse. But this result is representative of a completely uninformed choice. It will serve as a baseline against which to evaluate the performance of other more informed selections.

As mentioned before, the ranking-on-gain selection method is determined by simply choosing the projects with the best estimated gains until the budget money is exhausted. In this example the selected portfolio consists of projects 14, 15, 10, 8, 20, 6, and 18 for a total gain of

$$\$1622K + \$1144K + \$1048K + \$746K + \$610K + \$518K + \$494K = \$6182K$$

and a total cost of

$$\$13K + \$75K + \$24K + \$9K + \$10K + \$30K + \$26K = \$187K.$$

Clearly this selection method does better than the random method, producing a gain that is 100(6182 − 1420)/1420 = 335% better in its performance.

The integer programming approach determines the project portfolio with the highest gain possible within the budget cap and consists of projects 6, 7, 8, 10, 14, 15, 18, and 20. The total cost of this optimal project portfolio is

$$\$31K + \$6K + \$9K + \$24K + \$13K + \$75K \\ + \$30K + \$10K = \$198K.$$

Notice that there is a good deal of overlap with the ranking generated portfolio but the two are not nearly identical. The expected gain due to this portfolio is

$$\$518 + \$176 + \$746 + \$1048 + \$1622 + \$1144 \\ + \$494 + \$610 = \$6358.$$

This again is clearly better than the random portfolio but it is also better than the ranking selection. Specifically this integer programming solution is about $200K better or 100(6358 − 6182)/6182 = 3% better than the ranking-based portfolio. One should conclude that even in this simplest of all project selection scenarios, the programming method outperforms the simple ranked selection but that the gain is not dramatic. The gain can be dramatic as more constraints and complexities are imposed on the project selection.

PORTFOLIOS WITH RISK CONSTRAINTS

Now consider the addition of a risk constraint to the portfolio selection requirements. There is a choice inherent in the Six Sigma project selection mode to constrain risk either on the total portfolio or on each individual project itself. Since most current selection approaches do not really treat the projects as an integrated portfolio it is common to apply risk constraints on each project. Often this constraint is imposed by simply filtering out any project that does not meet a preestablished threshold of risk. Table 2.2 shows examples of the portfolios that might be generated with a risk constraint of 40 percent on each project. This requirement implies that projects 6, 10, and 13 are no longer acceptable and will not be considered in the portfolio.

Table 2.2 Risk-acceptable set of projects.

Project number	Gain in K$	Cost in K$	Percent risk
Project 1	94	20	15
Project 2	182	95	7
Project 3	76	66	24
Project 4	76	64	2
Project 5	68	12	7
Project 7	176	6	14
Project 8	746	9	15
Project 9	372	26	10
Project 11	254	47	40
Project 12	184	11	14
Project 14	1622	13	31
Project 15	1144	75	8
Project 16	120	29	40
Project 17	230	26	40
Project 18	494	30	36
Project 19	174	28	11

Based on this set of reduced projects, a representative random portfolio would be projects 2, 19, 1, and 12 which together achieve a cost of

$$95K + \$28K + \$20K + \$11K = \$154K$$

for an estimated gain of

$$\$182K + \$174K + \$94K + \$184K = \$634K.$$

The gain-ranked portfolio comprises projects 14, 15, 8, 18, 9, 11, and 17 with a cost of

$$\$13K + \$75K + \$9K + \$30K + \$26K + \$47K = \$200K$$

and an expected gain of

$$\$1622K + \$1144K + \$746K + \$494K + \$26K$$
$$+ \$47K + \$26K = \$4105K.$$

Notice that the imposition of the risk constraints reduced the portfolio value from $6182K to $4105K and prevented nearly two million dollars of benefit to accrue. It is normally much more difficult to find best portfolios when there are sets of constraints that must be respected. Again the ranking method has easily outperformed the random choice of projects, but how about the integer programming–generated solution? The integer programming portfolio for this risk-abbreviated list of projects consists of projects 7, 8, 9, 12, 14, 15, 17, and 18, with a total cost of

$$\$6K + \$9K + \$26K + \$11K + \$13K + \$75K + \$26K$$
$$+ \$30K = \$196K$$

and an expected gain of

$$\$176K + \$746K + \$372K + \$184K + \$1622K$$
$$+ \$1144K + \$230K + \$494K = \$4968K.$$

The linear programming (LP) solution is $100(4956 - 4105)/4105 = 21\%$ better and provides more than $700K extra in anticipated gain than the gain-ranked selection. Generally, as more constraints are added, the integer programming solution will extend its advantage ever more fully over the ranked method.

A better way to manage risk is to set a risk constraint on the average or total risk of the portfolio rather than on each individual project as is done in the standard method. If a target is set for the average risk of 40 percent, then the total risk should be $.40 * 10 = 4.00$. This very concept implies that the natural unit of performance is the portfolio rather than the individual project so it is usually not considered in standard Six Sigma project selection approaches. If one does apply this constraint on the portfolio risk, then the LP method is able to generate a much better portfolio by considering gain over the full set of 20 potential projects. This new integer programming portfolio consists of 6, 7, 8, 10, 14, 15, 18, and 20, with cost

$$= \$31K + \$6K + \$9K + \$24K + \$13K + \$75K$$
$$+ \$30K + \$10K = \$198K$$

and the expected gain due to this portfolio is

$$\$518 + \$176 + \$746 + \$1048 + \$1622 + \$1144$$
$$+ \$494 + \$610 = \$6358.$$

If one compares this portfolio risk method to the usual Six Sigma project-by-project selection process with a restriction applied to each project, then there is a much bigger gain of around $2200K of $100(6358 - 4105)/4105 = 55\%$ better!

In summary, the portfolio approach will always outperform (or at worst perform equally with) a collection of projects that are chosen independently. In real situations where there are a number of constraints that must be respected, the potential gain of the portfolio approach can be quite high and can substantially impact the overall success of the Six Sigma program.

3
Multiple Criteria Decision Making Methods for Six Sigma Project Selection

THE NEED FOR MULTIPLE CRITERIA

The standard Six Sigma project selection process that is described in Chapter 2 is simple enough to apply when there is only a single characteristic presented for each project but it becomes much more complicated when there are multiple project characteristics. Later chapters in this book that deal with programming methods will show ways to deal with these multiple characteristics as constraints, but this chapter and several that follow will treat these characteristics as objectives. These objectives may be equal in force or some may take on secondary importance to the others. In either case, these multiple objectives need to be balanced against one another as the selection process proceeds. As one might imagine, there are just as many ways to approach a multiple criteria problem as there are varieties of such problems. But there are a few good, generally applicable methods that fit right into Six Sigma project selection. Some of these methods belong to a set of techniques called *multiple criteria decision making* (MCDM) methods (Belton 2001), which are the subject of this chapter.

The MCDM methods discussed in this chapter will be of a restricted type in which multiple objectives are combined either by an assigned weighting scheme or by use of self-weighting generated by a Pareto principle. Each method will be first described generically with pointers given for fitting it into the Six Sigma project portfolio selection routine. Then a detailed example will be given that shows an application of the method. Some important features and cautions will be added to the discussion as they become pertinent.

CONVERSION OF MCDM TO A COMMON CRITERION

Consider the situation that one faces in the Six Sigma project selection process. There are a number of possible projects P each with C characteristics such as cost, benefit, customer importance, and so on. In multiple criteria decisions, each characteristic can provide an additional objective of the project. Some of the characteristics might need to be minimized rather than maximized and still others might require hitting a specific target. In most practical situations some of the multiple objectives will be completely contradictory and nearly all will be incompatible to some extent. Therefore it will be nearly impossible to achieve the optimum for each characteristic that might be possible if these conflicts did not exist. Consider Figure 3.1, which shows the relationship of two hypothetical characteristics called reliability and flexibility that vary as a function of the number of parts in a device. In this case, if the aim is maximize both objectives, then there is no single solution that will work. That is, no single value of number of parts will achieve maximums for A and B simultaneously. In a similar manner, it will not be possible, in general, to achieve a projects portfolio that optimizes all the desired characteristics.

One common approach to this problem of contradictory objectives is to assign some kind of conversion factor to each characteristic to achieve (at

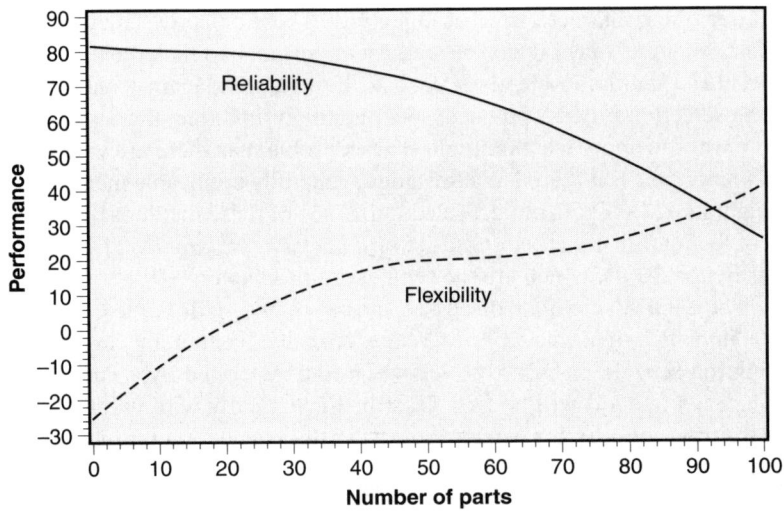

Figure 3.1 A contradictory relationship between two characteristics.

least approximately) a single scale. Often money is used for this purpose. That is, reliability in the previous example might be assigned a monetary value and the same for flexibility. The value of the system can be assumed to be a sum of the values for the two separate components. Then the optimization can be achieved by finding the maximum of this single valued objective. See Figure 3.2 for the component and total value relationships and how this can identify a best value.

Of course there are potential pitfalls in using this method. For one, there might not be an acceptable way in which to assign a common conversion. For example, one may have difficulty assessing the monetary value of a human life, or of corporate morale, or of customer loyalty. Another potential problem is with the assumption that the component values can be simply added together to get a meaningful value on which to base decision making. For example, it might be impossible to get more than three dollars for the product no matter how flexible and reliable it is. Marketplace considerations may put constraints on the two component value relationships and thereby change the way in which they add. The same kind of marketplace considerations might also place constraints on the ranges that are allowable for the two characteristics. See Figure 3.3 for an example of how these constraints may alter the choice of a best number of parts.

It is also possible that all the characteristics should not be weighted equally even if they have a common conversion. For example, process

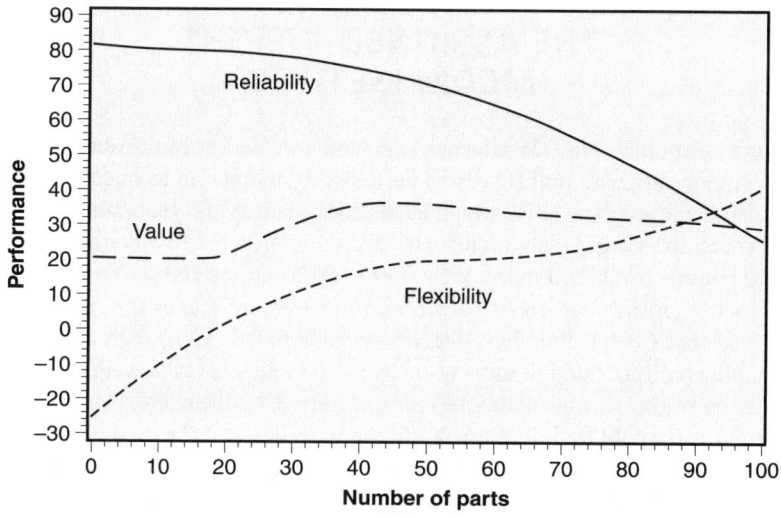

Figure 3.2   A nonlinear relationship between two characteristics.

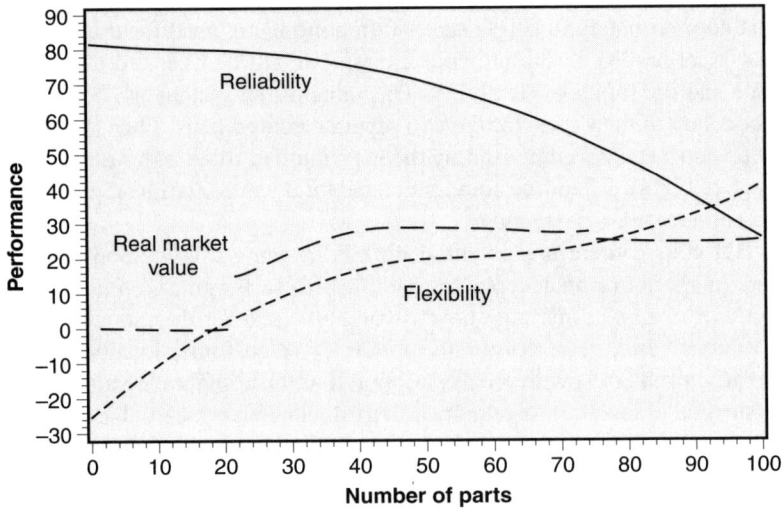

Figure 3.3 A relationship between characteristics with constraints.

complexity may only account for a small financial gain but needs to be included in the decision only after the major profit objective is satisfied. Thus there might be a natural hierarchy to the multiple criteria.

THE ASSIGNED-WEIGHT MCDM METHOD

There is another MCDM alternative to the conversion of all objectives to a common attribute that serves as an index allowing one to make a proper decision although a not truly measurable quantity is generated. In this approach the multiple characteristics are not converted to a common attribute but are combined more or less arbitrarily into an index. This index is a function of the characteristics whose improvement makes the right trade-offs so that overall the right decision is made. This index can be a quite complicated function but most of the time the index is just a weighted combination of the various characteristics. Figure 3.4 shows what such a functional form might look like for the C characteristics of the example.

The weights that determine the index can be fitted from observed data if it is available. In the stock market, for example, one might track the average of all stock returns against the return of a weighted average of a few individual stocks. If this tracking is stable through time, then it might be a

Multiple Criteria Decision Making Methods for Six Sigma Project Selection 29

$$\text{Index} = \text{constant} + wt_1 * \text{attribute}_1 + wt_2 * \text{attribute}_2 + \ldots + wt_c * \text{attribute}_c$$

Figure 3.4 A functional relationship between project characteristics.

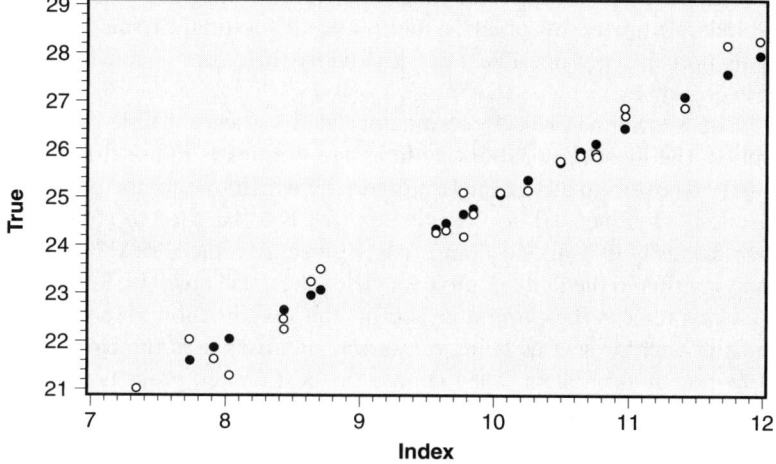

Figure 3.5 The possible fit of an index to project characteristics.

useful way in which to choose the weights for the linear combination. Multiple linear regression is a procedure that is often applied to fit these weights when there is adequate and suitable data. See Figure 3.5 for an example of such an index approach.

In the application of MCDM to Six Sigma project portfolio selection such a choice of weights is a little more problematic. But it should be possible in some cases to show that a certain choice of weights seems to match up well with successful project results over time. What is probably most important for the assignment of weights is that they seem fair to all the participants. Thus, it is often possible to produce the set of weights through a group process in which one starts with equal weighting of all characteristics and then allows discussion on possible modifications to the weights. This process continues until a consensus is reached and a final set of weights is chosen. This set of weights may not be optimal in the sense of achieving the absolute maximum performance but at least it is consistent and acceptable to the selection committee. There are also group decision processes that can be used to assimilate individual preferences into an overall weight that accurately portrays the behavior of the group as a single individual.

APPLICATION OF ASSIGNED WEIGHTS TO A SIMPLE PROBLEM

Consider the application of assigned weights to a simple project portfolio problem in which there are 20 projects and three characteristics of cost, benefit, and risk. Clearly cost should be minimized, benefit maximized, and risk minimized to achieve a multi-attribute optimal choice. Intuitively this is probably not possible since it is likely that there is conflict among these objectives.

The Six Sigma project coordinator decides ahead of time that, in her opinion, the most reasonable way to assign weights is to use the expected benefit to cost ratio as the single measure by which to rank the projects for selection. This means that the function that is to be used to combine the three elements of gain, cost, and risk is given as value = risk * gain/cost. Applying this to the table of projects yields the data shown in Table 3.1.

Upon review, the committee accepts this combination of the three elements of each project as being reasonable and uses it as the basic sorting of the potential projects. They choose the best-ranked projects under this new scheme and fund as many as they can fit within the total budget cap of $200K. The Six Sigma project portfolio achieved in this MCDM assigned-weight approach consists of the projects 14, 20, 10, 8, 6, 18, 13, 7, 17, and 12. This portfolio would have predicted total gain of $6060K, total cost of $174K, and risk per project of 58 percent.

PARETO-OPTIMAL APPROACHES IN MCDM

Although it was portrayed in the previous section as an easy decision to accept the proposed combination of the three project properties, it is often difficult for the selection committee to agree on the proper assigned weights. One of the reasons for this difficulty is the fact that it is hard to define what optimal means for a vector of values. In these situations it may be much better to generate the weights by applying a different kind of logic. This can be done by searching for a Pareto-optimal Six Sigma project portfolio. A Pareto-optimal solution (Raphael 2003) is a set of projects none of which are dominated by any other potential project. A dominated project is one that has less gain, more cost, and higher probability of failure than some other specific project. Consider Figure 3.6, which illustrates a set of dominated projects by black dots and nondominated projects by open dots when the projects have only two characteristics: cost and benefit.

Table 3.1 The weighted value index of the simple problem.

Project number	Gain in K$	Cost in K$	Percent risk	Value
Project 1	94	20	15	71
Project 2	182	95	7	13
Project 3	76	66	24	28
Project 4	76	64	2	2
Project 5	68	12	7	40
Project 6	518	31	42	702
Project 7	176	6	14	411
Project 8	746	9	15	1243
Project 9	372	26	10	143
Project 10	1048	24	44	1921
Project 11	254	47	40	216
Project 12	184	11	14	234
Project 13	178	14	44	559
Project 14	1622	13	31	3868
Project 15	1144	75	8	122
Project 16	120	29	40	166
Project 17	230	26	40	354
Project 18	494	30	36	593
Project 19	174	28	11	68
Project 20	610	10	46	2806

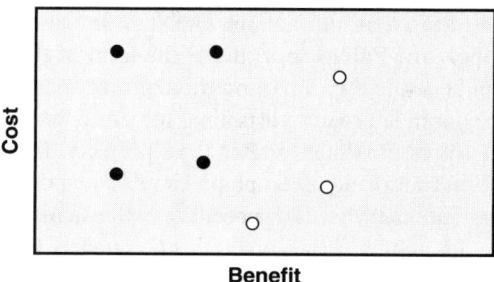

Figure 3.6 An example of dominance in two variables.

It seems reasonable that such dominated projects should not be part of an optimized portfolio. After all, they are poorer than some other choice in every possible characteristic. Notice that a Pareto-optimal project portfolio depends on which characteristics are selected for ranking. It is generally much more difficult to find simple Pareto-optimal sets as the number of characteristics increases.

APPLICATION OF THE PARETO MCDM APPROACH TO A COMPLEX EXAMPLE

Consider the case of 20 projects that was used as an example in Chapter 2. For this example there will be three characteristics under consideration, so a project will be considered dominated if it has lower gain, higher cost, and higher percentage failure risk than some other potential projects in the list. The full set is shown in Table 3.2.

With a little effort and sorting on the three columns of gain, cost, and risk, it is possible to check for the full set of dominated projects. For example, compare project L and project M as shown in Table 3.3.

Project L has higher gain of $50K versus $16K for project M. Similarly, project L has a cost of $4.0K, which is less than the cost for project M, which is $8.0K. And finally, risk for project L is 35, which is less than the 40 for project M. Therefore, project L dominates project M, and project M can be removed from the list of potential projects.

DOMINATED PORTFOLIOS

The dominance relation that was applied in the previous section was handled at the level of the project. In this mode one compares pairs of projects in order to isolate the Pareto-optimal set. But it is just as feasible and probably better to apply the Pareto checking at the level of the whole portfolio. That is, one can generate a group of possible project portfolios. One might construct all 10 possible project portfolios, for example, and search for the Pareto-optimal set of portfolios rather than projects. In order to identify this Pareto-optimal portfolio, one compares pairs of portfolios rather than pairs of projects but otherwise the procedure is the same as outlined above. Consider Table 3.4, which shows projects J through N from the full table. One can use this smaller set of projects to illustrate the process of obtaining a Pareto-optimal set of Six Sigma project portfolios.

Table 3.2 A realistic set of projects with more constraints.

Project name	Gain $100K	Cost $100K	% failure	Directive	Training
Project A	2	0.3	25	1	GB
Project C	10	0.3	12	2	GB
Project D	8	0.2	5	2, 3	BB
Project E	25	5.0	50	1, 2, 3	MBB
Project F	5	1.0	5	3	BB
Project G	5	0.8	10	3	GB
Project H	7	0.2	25	2	BB
Project J	11	0.7	35	1	GB
Project K	4	1.0	25	1	GB
Project L	50	4.0	35	3	MBB
Project M	16	8.0	40	1, 2	BB
Project N	26	1.2	70	1, 3	MBB
Project P	1	0.2	70	3	GB
Project Q	3	0.3	37	1	BB
Project R	8	0.8	25	1	BB
Project S	5	0.8	12	2	GB
Project T	5	1.8	3	1	GB
Project U	22	10.0	18	2, 3	BB
Project V	38	10.0	80	1, 2, 3	MBB
Project W	9	0.9	40	1, 3	BB

Table 3.3 A subset of the full set of potential projects.

Project name	Gain	Cost	Risk
Project L	50	4.0	35
Project M	16	8.0	40

Table 3.4 Another subset of the full project listing.

Project name	Gain $100K	Cost $100K	% Failure
Project J	11	0.7	35
Project K	4	1.0	25
Project L	50	4.0	35
Project M	16	8.0	40

Table 3.5 The possible two-project portfolios for the subset.

Project name	Gain	Cost	Risk
J and K	15	1.7	60
J and L	61	4.7	60
J and M	27	8.7	75
K and L	54	5.0	60
K and M	20	9.0	65
L and M	66	12.0	75

This set can be used to construct six different two-project portfolios. The gain, cost, and risk for each two-project portfolio can be constructed by summing the individual projects. Table 3.5 shows the results for each possible two-project portfolio formed in this way.

Upon examination, one can see that the K and L portfolio dominates all other portfolios except the portfolio containing projects J and K and the portfolio containing projects L and M. Therefore the potential projects would be reduced to the three portfolios JK, LM, and KL. Although this seems clear enough and even relatively easy to apply to this reduced set of projects, it is decidedly not easy to apply when there are many projects. For example, even with the reduced set of projects given in Table 3.4, the problem becomes much harder if one considers all project portfolios rather than just the two-project portfolios. There are six one-project portfolios, 15 two-project portfolios, 20 three-project portfolios, 20 four-project portfolios, 15 five-project portfolios, and one six-project portfolio. Adding all these portfolios together would yield 77 different individual cases to check for the Pareto-optimal set. Checking all pairs of these 77 would mean 77 * 76 = 5652 pairs that might need to be checked in this process.

Clearly even a small set of potential projects can lead to a large number of pairs of project portfolios to check in the process of finding the Pareto-optimal set of portfolios, but the problem becomes nearly unmanageable when realistic scenarios are considered. For example, with 20 potential projects there are 20!/2!18! = 190 two-project portfolios to consider rather than just the six that were available for the simplistic six-project example. And there are 184,756 10-project portfolios to consider. Accounting for all possible project portfolios in this 20-project example there are 1,048,575 total project portfolios to consider in the search for the best set. Within this 20-project scenario there are 549,754,241,025 pairs of project portfolios to consider in the search process! Modern computers equipped with the right programs may be able to handle even these enormous numbers, but it is more likely that one will need to presort the possible portfolios to reduce the number of candidates before continuing the search. For example, only feasible projects might first be selected. Then one might argue that the bigger portfolios are to be preferred so one might only search portfolios between some minimum size and the largest feasible size. This would restrict the number of pairs of project portfolios greatly and probably enable, with some extensive number crunching, arriving at the Pareto-optimal Six Sigma project portfolio.

RECIPES FOR THE METHODS USED IN THIS CHAPTER

MCDM

Step 1 Assign weights to all the objectives (these weights can be derived from first principles, from fitting to data, or by arbitrary consensus by the project selection team)

Step 2 Multiply the weights by the project characteristic values to create a single index value that represents the cumulative effect of all objectives

Step 3 Select projects based on their ranks according to this index value

Pareto-Optimal

Step 1 Test for dominance of every project (portfolio) by pair-wise comparisons of it with the other projects (portfolios)

Step 2 Select projects (portfolios) for final portfolio by ranking within this Pareto-optimal set of nondominated projects (portfolios)

4

The Analytic Hierarchy Approach to Project Portfolio Selection

THE PROBLEM WITH ASSIGNED WEIGHTS

The ranking method described in Chapter 3 is one way to apply multiple-criteria decision making to the project portfolio selection problem. The original method that was presented requires the assignment of weights to the various decision factors such as cost, benefit, and risk. This means that often it is impossible to apply the method in a group setting wherein no consensus can be achieved. Situations in which no true consensus can be reached are probably quite common when the selection committee is constituted from a peer group of managers. Often each manager is trying to make organizational points and protect his or her turf as much as trying to achieve an efficient portfolio. Even in other situations in which organizational politics does not play a dominant role, there can be technical reasons why some team members feel that they can not assign appropriate weights in the process.

Another potential difficulty in applying the assigned weights is that they are easy to manipulate. A savvy manager or bloc of managers may be able to see a way to assign the weights in such a way that their projects are more likely to be selected by the MCDM process. All methods are probably susceptible to some tampering of this nature but much of the danger is removed by self-generated weights. As an example of how such manipulation might occur, reconsider the first example considered in Chapter 3 under the heading Complex Example with Assigned Weights. A manager who understands the process may try to influence it her way by choosing weights that favor her projects. If one of her projects has an unusually high level of risk then she can try to ensure that a small weight is placed on risk in the overall computation of the index. In this way she can influence the process for reasons not directly related to the merits of the individual projects.

To avoid these problems it is possible to generate the weights in an objective fashion based on the *analytic hierarchy process,* or AHP for short (Saaty 1980). The methodology of the AHP is not extremely different from that of the MCDM of Chapter 3 but the weights are generated in a more algorithmic fashion. The process proceeds in three steps and there is a way to check for consistency of the process as well. The generic procedure will be presented and then two applications will be made. The first application will be the simple three-factor problem that was used above to motivate the need for the AHP and the second will be the more complicated example presented later in Chapter 4.

THE AHP PROCEDURE

Consider the generic project portfolio selection problem. Assume that there are P projects to be rated on C characteristics. These characteristics might be cost, benefit, risk, and other features of the projects that are of importance to the committee. The purpose is to rank the projects in such a way that the weights used to combine the multiple characteristics into one decision can be assigned automatically. The AHP uses pair-wise comparisons to generate this automatic combination of the individual conflicting objectives.

Step one of the AHP is to rank the pairs of projects against one another on a nine-point scale where 1 = equally preferred and 9 = extremely preferred for each characteristic separately. Given a set of P projects there are $P!/2!(P-2)!$ unique pairs that must be examined for each of m characteristics. Full details of the procedure will be given in the examples below but for now simply assume that the preferences are given $p(i,j)$ where i and j run from 1 to n. Notice that if project a is preferred to project b by a rating of 4 then it is assumed for consistency that project b is preferred to project a with a factor of 1/4. Thus all possible pair-wise rankings can be generated from the unique ones. Also note that by definition the rating of the system with itself is equal to 1.

Step two consists of normalizing the resulting rankings so that the sum of entries for each project and for each characteristic equals 1. This constraint of summation to one makes the resulting values look like probabili-

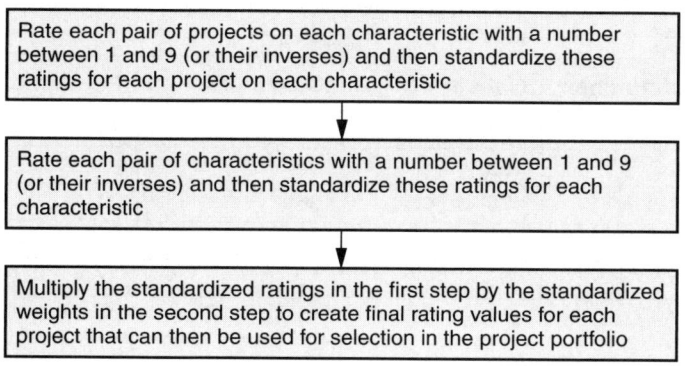

Figure 4.1 The steps in applying AHP.

ties. It is these probabilities that give one a way to automatically combine the objectives. The detailed example below will demonstrate this process more clearly.

The third step repeats steps one and two for each pair-wise consideration of the C characteristics themselves rather than the P projects. The normalization of these ratings is the self-generated weights for combining the normalized ratings generated by steps one and two applied to the projects. The final application then results in a combined rating for each project across all characteristics using the self-generated weights. Typically, the project with the largest such final rating is selected for funding. One may use this set of rankings to select several projects until the funding is exhausted or the rankings can be used as inputs for the more sophisticated programming methods to be covered in later chapters. Figure 4.1 illustrates the steps to be used in applying AHP.

A SIMPLE AHP APPLICATION

As a start, one can consider the application of AHP to a reduced version of the 20-project Six Sigma portfolio selection process where there are only five projects, as shown in Table 4.1, with three characteristics of cost, benefit, and risk. With only five projects, there are $5!/3!2! = 10$ pairs to which the selection committee must assign weights between 1 and 9. Table 4.1 shows the information for the five projects. Table 4.2 shows the relative assignment of the weights to the 10 pairs for the gain characteristic and Table 4.3 shows the standardized weights.

Table 4.1 A subset of the full project listing.

Project number	Gain in K$	Cost in K$	Percent risk
Project 1	94	20	15
Project 2	182	95	7
Project 3	76	66	24
Project 4	76	64	2
Project 5	68	12	7

Table 4.2 Relative pair-wise rankings of the subset of projects.

Projects	1	2	3	4	5
1	1	1/7	2	2	5
2	7	1	5	5	6
3	1/2	1/5	1	1	2
4	1/2	1/5	1	1	2
5	1/5	1/6	1/2	1/2	1

Table 4.3 The standardized weights for gain.

Projects	1	2	3	4	5	Value
1	0.11	0.09	0.22	0.22	0.33	0.20
2	0.78	0.65	0.56	0.56	0.40	**0.59**
3	0.06	0.13	0.11	0.11	0.13	0.11
4	0.06	0.13	0.11	0.11	0.13	0.11
5	0.02	0.11	0.06	0.06	0.07	0.06
Sum	9	154	9	9	15	

The same process then can be applied to the cost and risk characteristics for each pair-wise comparison of the five candidate Six Sigma projects. Tables 4.4 and 4.5 show in detail the standardized weights for each of these other two characteristics.

Finally the same process is applied to the ranking of the three characteristics of gain, cost, and risk themselves as shown in Table 4.6.

With all these weights at hand, the final choice is determined by multiplying each standardized weight characteristic for each project times the

Table 4.4 Standardized weights for cost.

Projects	1	2	3	4	5	Value
1	0.05	0.08	0.02	0.02	0.10	0.05
2	0.39	0.62	0.72	0.63	0.45	**0.56**
3	0.29	0.12	0.14	0.21	0.20	0.19
4	0.24	0.10	0.07	0.11	0.20	0.15
5	0.02	0.07	0.04	0.03	0.05	0.04
Sum	20.5	1.6	6.92	9.45	20	

Table 4.5 Standardized weights for risk.

Projects	1	2	3	4	5	Value
1	0.042857	0.046392	0.1	0.056338	0.02	0.053117
2	0.214286	0.231959	0.3	0.253521	0.16	0.231953
3	0.014286	0.025773	0.033333	0.056338	0.02	0.029946
4	0.385714	0.463918	0.3	0.507042	0.64	**0.459335**
5	0.342857	0.231959	0.266667	0.126761	0.16	0.225649
Sum	23.33	4.31	30	1.97	6.25	

Table 4.6 Standardized weights for the project characteristics.

	Gain	Cost	Risk
Gain	0.285714	0.285714	0.285714
Cost	0.142857	0.142857	0.142857
Risk	0.571429	0.571429	0.571429
Sum	3.5	7	1.75

standardized weights in order to combine them into one index. For example, for project 1 the standardized gain value is 0.20, the standardized cost value is 0.05, and the standardized risk is 0.053. These are multiplied by the standardized weights for their respective characteristics to give a final index 0.29 * 0.20 + 0.14 * 0.05 + 0.57 * 0.053 = 0.095. In this way the final ranking can be computed for each project as shown in Table 4.7. From this table it is project 2 that would be most highly ranked, and the ranking of all five projects would be 2–4–5–1–3.

Table 4.7 The AHP ranking of the subset of projects.

Project	Gain	Cost	Risk	Sum
1	0.054963	0.007617	0.030277	0.092857
2	0.164474	0.079015	0.132213	0.375703
3	0.030281	0.027263	0.017069	0.074614
4	0.030281	0.020328	0.261821	0.31243
5	0.017249	0.005777	0.12862	0.151646

Table 4.8 A subset of the two-project portfolios.

Project name	Gain	Cost	Risk
J and K	15	1.7	60
J and L	61	4.7	60
J and M	27	8.7	75
K and L	54	5.0	60
K and M	20	9.0	65
L and M	66	12.0	75

AN AHP EXAMPLE ON PORTFOLIOS

Just as in Chapter 3 where it was possible to apply the MCDM methods to projects or portfolios, it is also a good idea to apply AHP to whole portfolios rather than projects. Consider again the example of four projects given in Chapter 3 where there are only six two-project portfolios to consider. Consider Table 4.8, which repeats these six project portfolios.

In the same way, the project team can be asked to assign relative rankings to these Six Sigma project portfolios as complete entities in their own right. In many situations and for many teams this might be an easier task than the ranking of individual projects since it allows people to make judgments about the interactions of projects and balancing of priorities across several activities. On the other hand, especially in circumstances in which there are many nearly equal projects, this method can potentially be more difficult to apply to a conclusion.

Table 4.9 shows the original rankings assigned by the project team to the six project portfolios based on gain. Table 4.10 then shows the standardized rankings for the same gain characteristic. Tables 4.11 and 4.12

Table 4.9 Raw pair-wise rankings of the project portfolios for gain.

Portfolios	JK	JL	JM	KL	KM	LM
JK	1	0.166667	0.5	0.25	1	0.166667
JL	6	1	3	1	3	1
JM	2	0.333333	1	0.5	2	0.33
KL	4	1	2	1	4	0.5
KM	1	0.333333	0.5	0.25	1	0.33
LM	6	1	3	2	3	1
	20	3.833333	10	5	14	3.326667

Table 4.10 Standardized rankings of the project portfolios for gain.

Portfolios	JK	JL	JM	KL	KM	LM	Value
JK	0.05	0.043478	0.05	0.05	0.071429	0.0501	0.052501
JL	0.3	0.26087	0.3	0.2	0.214286	0.300601	0.262626
JM	0.1	0.086957	0.1	0.1	0.142857	0.099198	0.104835
KL	0.2	0.26087	0.2	0.2	0.285714	0.150301	0.216147
KM	0.05	0.086957	0.05	0.05	0.071429	0.099198	0.067931
LM	0.3	0.26087	0.3	0.4	0.214286	0.300601	0.295959

Table 4.11 Standardized rankings of the project portfolios for cost.

Portfolios	JK	JL	JM	KL	KM	LM	Value
JK	0.549259	0.6	0.488486	0.612745	0.489796	0.409091	0.524896
JL	0.109852	0.12	0.139567	0.122549	0.163265	0.136364	0.131933
JM	0.078466	0.06	0.069784	0.040441	0.081633	0.136364	0.077781
KL	0.109852	0.12	0.209351	0.122549	0.163265	0.181818	0.151139
KM	0.091543	0.06	0.069784	0.040441	0.081633	0.090909	0.072385
LM	0.061029	0.04	0.023029	0.061275	0.020408	0.045455	0.041866

show the standardized rankings for cost and risk. Notice that this last table is identical to the table used for projects in the previous section since it is assumed that the attitudes of the managers probably would not depend on whether the ranking was to be done on projects or on project portfolios.

Table 4.12 Standardized rankings of the project portfolios for risk.

Portfolios	JK	JL	JM	KL	KM	LM	Value
JK	0.25	0.129032	0.235294	0.25	0.255428	0.25	0.228292
JL	0.25	0.129032	0.235294	0.25	0.255428	0.25	0.228292
JM	0.0625	0.032258	0.058824	0.0625	0.042146	0.0625	0.053455
KL	0.25	0.129032	0.235294	0.25	0.255428	0.25	0.228292
KM	0.125	0.064516	0.176471	0.125	0.127714	0.125	0.12395
LM	0.0625	0.516129	0.058824	0.0625	0.063857	0.0625	0.137718

Table 4.13 The final AHP rankings for the portfolios.

Portfolio	Gain	Cost	Risk	Value
JK	0.052501	0.524896	0.228292	0.220438
JL	0.262626	0.131933	0.228292	0.224336
JM	0.104835	0.077781	0.053455	0.07161
KL	0.216147	0.151139	0.228292	0.2138
KM	0.067931	0.072385	0.12395	0.100578
LM	0.295959	0.041866	0.137718	0.169237

Finally with all these standardized weights at hand it is possible to compute a final rating for each of the six project portfolios that combines the information across the three characteristics. Table 4.13 shows the complete set of computations for the full set of six potential Six Sigma project portfolios. From this table it is clear that the portfolio containing projects J and L is narrowly ranked highest over the portfolio with projects J and K in this AHP approach.

PROBLEMS WITH THE AHP APPROACH

The AHP approach has many advantages, especially in that it generates the weights in an objective fashion once the pair-wise rankings are made. But there are some disadvantages as well. The examples in the previous section considered only a small number of possible projects; a larger number of projects can cause numerical and tactical problems. For the case of five projects there were 10 pairs of projects to consider. But for 20 possible Six

Sigma projects there would be 190 pairs to consider. It is not really difficult to handle the standardization process or to compute the final values for each project but it is difficult for the project team to rank so many pairs with any type of consistency. Indeed it would be almost impossible to get even the managerial time or attention to rank so many pairs.

The same problem occurs in the case of AHP application to entire project portfolios only the problem is even more pronounced. In the example of four projects there were a total of six possible two-project portfolios to consider. With 20 projects there would be 190 possible two-project portfolios. This would be of the same degree of difficulty for a project selection committee to manage as it was in the case of individual projects. But consider now that there are also one-project portfolios to consider and there are 20 of these. And there are 20 * 19 * 18/3 * 2 = 1040 possible three-project portfolios and even more four- and five-project portfolios. The number increases until 10-project portfolios are considered and then decreases again until one gets to the 20-project portfolios, of which there is only one. Clearly this is an impossible task for any practical application, So unless some preliminary sorting is done, the AHP method is not to be recommended for application to large-project problems unless some kind of automatic ranking can be done.

RECIPE FOR THE METHOD USED IN THIS CHAPTER

AHP

Step 1 Assign rankings to all pair-wise comparisons of projects (portfolios) with numbers between 1 and 9 (or their inverses)

Step 2 Standardize these rankings by dividing by the row totals

Step 3 Assign rankings to all pair-wise comparisons of the multiple characteristics with numbers between 1 and 9 (or their inverses)

Step 4 Standardize these weights by dividing by the row totals

Step 5 Multiply standardized ratings by standardized weights to form an index value that can be used to assign projects (portfolios) to the final portfolio

5
The Data Envelopment Approach to Six Sigma Portfolio Selection

AN EXTENSION OF THE MCDM PARETO METHOD

Chapter 3 introduced the Pareto-optimal MCDM method for the creation of Six Sigma project portfolios—the bedrock on which one can construct more advanced methods that can make the choice of weights less subjective. This can be important in situations in which management has difficulty in reaching a consensus because of their differing perspectives on the projects. This chapter will present another one of these methods, called *data envelopment analysis* or DEA, that can obtain the weights in an objective manner. The DEA method uses a ranking and weighting scheme that is based on the characteristics of the projects themselves and does not require any overt specification of probabilities or preferences (Ray 2004). Unlike the AHP procedure, the DEA method finds a valuable way to combine the objectives based on comparison of the project characteristics themselves. It does this by constructing a possibly fictitious project that represents the optimal way to get performance out of the project resources. This constructed project can then serve as a baseline or reference for comparison of the actual proposed projects. The DEA method is widely used in econometrics to rank and estimate the efficiencies of business units. This chapter will take advantage of just a few of the potential applications of DEA to the selection of Six Sigma projects.

To better understand the process of DEA, one must become more familiar with the meaning of the baseline project. The baseline project is formulated as what econometricians call an efficient horizon. The horizon is fundamentally a geometrical construction around the set of projects that serves as an envelope containing all hypothetical projects that can be formed as convex combinations of the individual projects. The horizon serves as a boundary that can be equaled but not exceeded by any individual project. This horizon provides two useful properties that can be defined for each project. First of all, since the horizon project is a weighted combination of the individual projects, it gives a natural way in which to compute the combining weights. Secondly, the distance from each individual project to the reference provides a measure of the suboptimality of that project and points to ways in which it can be improved.

A simple example will be used to demonstrate the construction and application of the DEA horizon for a set of projects. Consider a simple two-project scenario in which project A can be funded at $10K for an expected gain of $80K and project B can be funded at $20K for an expected gain of $100K. If there is a cap on spending that only permits a total expenditure of $15K, then the optimal portfolio was shown in Chapter 2 to consist of a strategy of fully funding project A at $10k and putting the remaining $5K into project B for a gain of $105K. This optimal funding plan is hypothetical in this case because projects usually have to be fully funded or not funded at all. In this simple case this hypothetical portfolio can serve as the reference project and can be used as the boundary to which one can compare each of the projects A and B.

The expected gain of a portfolio that fully funds only project A is $80K. The distance from this single project portfolio to the hypothetical ideal situation is $105K − $80K = $25K. Or one may express this by saying that project A is 100 * $80K / $105K = 70% efficient. In the same way, project B can be considered to be 100 * $75K / $105K = 71% efficient. Basically this is a measure of how efficient each project is at achieving the best value at the efficient frontier. Although this example concentrates on gain to help one understand the process, the general DEA analysis can handle multiple characteristics just as easily. Figure 5.1 illustrates a possible envelope or horizon for several projects with just two characteristics.

Turning from this simple example back to practical application, one must face at least two new challenges. For one thing, real project selection tasks can include more complex sets of characteristics in the computations. This is complicated enough that it becomes almost mandatory to use a computer to construct the DEA reference project. The most effective way in which to use the computer to do this construction is through the use of linear programming code. The details of linear programming will be given in Chapter 6 but in this chapter the method will simply be used to do the construction. Remember that the primary objective of this DEA approach to Six Sigma project portfolio selection is to provide a justifiable prioritization to each project in a less subjective way than was provided by most of

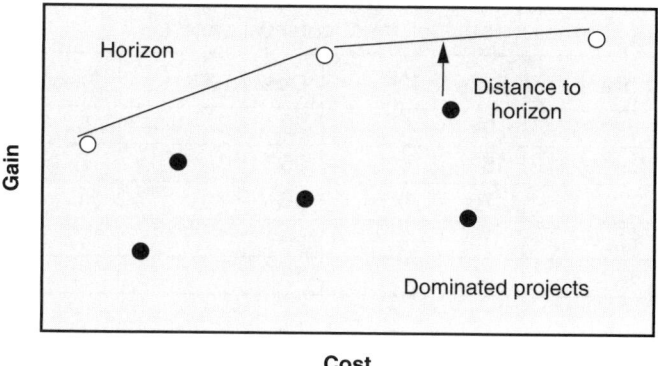

Figure 5.1 An illustration of the data envelope or horizon.

the methods presented in Chapters 3 and 4. These efficiencies do not have a strict interpretation in the economic sense but they can provide a valid way to prioritize projects.

The linear programming method requires software that can solve each construction in an efficient manner since there must be a separate run of the code for each project that is considered in the portfolio. Fortunately there are many good linear programming applications that will do the job adequately for most realistic Six Sigma portfolio selection problems. This text will use the SAS system but almost any linear programming code can be used to solve the problem by copying the code given here or by accessing the Ray reference given above. The SAS LP implementation presented here will automatically create the data envelope, compute distances from projects, indicate improvement opportunities, and provide an indication a of problem with the procedure.

A SIMPLE LP DEA EXAMPLE

An introductory example is provided by the abbreviated five-project list shown in Table 5.1 that is an extraction from the full set of 20 potential projects used earlier.

Figure 5.2 shows the linear programming code that will solve this DEA problem for project 1 as it is given in Table 5.1. This code is a modification of the code given for DEA in (Ray 2004). The code will be almost identical to the code that is used in further application to the other four projects. The SAS software requires that one first create a data set called

Table 5.1 A subset of the full set of potential projects.

Project number	Gain in K$	Cost in K$	Percent risk
Project 1	94	20	15
Project 2	182	95	7
Project 3	76	66	24
Project 4	76	64	2
Project 5	68	12	7

```
data deabook;
input _id_ $ p1 p2 p3 p4 p5 phi _type_ $ _rhs_;
cards;
obj 0 0 0 0 0 1 max .
gain 94 182 76 74 68 -94 ge 0
cost 20 95 66 64 12 0 le 20
risk 15 7 24 2 7 0 le 15
;
proc lp data=deabook;
run;
```

Figure 5.2 The code for the first DEA project analysis.

"deabook" in this code. Then the *proc lp* section of code works on this data set to create output in either text or data set format. The text output will be used exclusively for the examples in this book. The reader is referred to the SAS manual section on the LP procedure contained in the Operations Research User's Guide (SAS Institute 1989) for any additional details. However, it should be reasonably clear that the input statement assigns the project names and the keywords that define the actions that are taken on each line of input. For example the line marked "obj" defines the function to be maximized while the other lines treat the gain cost and risks of the projects. The inputs columns must line up with the input statement so that correct assignments of gain, cost, and risk are matched with the project names.

Once this code is constructed, the computation of the efficiency of each project becomes almost trivial. For example, the efficiency of project 1 is given by the inverse of the optimal phi value given in the output times 100. Since the output (Figure 5.3) shows that this optimal phi value is equal to 1.2056738, the efficiency is 82.9 percent. The output also shows the details of the construction of the baseline project as project 5 funded at

```
                         The LP Procedure
                         Variable Summary
         Variable                                              Reduced
    Col  Name      Status  Type       Price    Activity        Cost
      1  p1                NON-NEG        0           0        -0.205674
      2  p2                NON-NEG        0           0        -3.79078
      3  p3                NON-NEG        0           0        -3.170213
      4  p4                NON-NEG        0           0        -3.070922
      5  p5        BASIC   NON-NEG        0    1.6666667               0
      6  phi       BASIC   NON-NEG        1    1.2056738               0
      7  gain              SURPLUS        0           0        -0.010638
      8  cost              SLACK          0           0        -0.060284
      9  risk      BASIC   SLACK          0    3.3333333               0
```

Figure 5.3 The output for the first DEA project analysis.

```
data deabook;
input _id_ $ p1 p2 p3 p4 p5 phi _type_ $ _rhs_;
cards;
obj 0 0 0 0 0 1 max .
gain 94 182 76 74 68 -182 ge 0
cost 20 95 66 64 12 0 le 95
risk 15 7 24 2 7 0 le 7
;
title 'project 2';
proc lp data=deabook;
run;
```

Figure 5.4 The code for the second DEA project analysis.

1.67 its nominal amount. In addition, the existence of a nonzero slack value for this project shows that the efficiency can be increased by lowering its risk. Thus the LP solution to DEA provides what is needed for Six Sigma project prioritization as well as additional information that might be profitably used in the validation of the individual projects themselves.

In order to make sure that the method is clear before a more complete application example is done, the details of the program code and the solution will be given for each of the other four projects in the abbreviated portfolio example. Figures 5.4 and 5.5 show the program and the output for project 2, Figures 5.6 and 5.7 for project 3, Figures 5.8 and 5.9 for project 4, and Figures 5.10 and 5.11 complete the survey with project 5. Finally, the efficiencies and reference projects are summarized for convenience for each of the five individual projects in Table 5.2.

52 Chapter Five

```
project 2
                     The LP Procedure
                      Variable Summary
      Variable                                         Reduced
Col   Name     Status  Type       Price   Activity      Cost
  1   p1               NON-NEG        0        0      -0.241021
  2   p2       BASIC   NON-NEG        0        1            0
  3   p3               NON-NEG        0        0      -1.051011
  4   p4               NON-NEG        0        0      -0.15727
  5   p5       DEGEN   NON-NEG        0        0            0
  6   phi      BASIC   NON-NEG        1        1            0
  7   gain             SURPLUS        0        0      -0.005495
  8   cost             SLACK          0        0      -0.007547
  9   risk             SLACK          0        0      -0.040438
```

Figure 5.5 The output for the second DEA project analysis.

```
data deabook;
input _id_ $ p1 p2 p3 p4 p5 phi _type_ $ _rhs_;
cards;
obj 0 0 0 0 0 1 max .
gain 94 182 76 74 68 -76 ge 0
cost 20 95 66 64 12 0 le 66
risk 15 7 24 2 7 0 le 24
;
title 'project 3';
proc lp data=deabook;
run;
```

Figure 5.6 The code for the third DEA project analysis.

```
project 3
                     The LP Procedure
                      Variable Summary
      Variable                                         Reduced
Col   Name     Status  Type       Price   Activity      Cost
  1   p1               NON-NEG        0        0      -0.577181
  2   p2       BASIC   NON-NEG        0   0.2994836          0
  3   p3               NON-NEG        0        0      -2.516895
  4   p4               NON-NEG        0        0      -0.376619
  5   p5       BASIC   NON-NEG        0   3.1290878          0
  6   phi      BASIC   NON-NEG        1   3.5168946          0
  7   gain             SURPLUS        0        0      -0.013158
  8   cost             SLACK          0        0      -0.018072
  9   risk             SLACK          0        0      -0.096838
```

Figure 5.7 The output for the third DEA project analysis.

The Data Envelopment Approach to Six Sigma Portfolio Selection 53

```
data deabook;
input _id_ $ p1 p2 p3 p4 p5 phi _type_ $ _rhs_;
cards;
obj 0 0 0 0 0 1 max .
gain 94 182 76 74 68 -74 ge 0
cost 20 95 66 64 12 0 le 64
risk 15 7 24 2 7 0 le 2
;
title 'project 4';
proc lp data=deabook;
run;
```

Figure 5.8 The code for the fourth DEA project analysis.

```
                        The LP Procedure
                        Variable Summary

      Variable                                              Reduced
Col   Name      Status   Type        Price   Activity       Cost
 1    p1                 NON-NEG       0         0         -2.519275
 2    p2        DEGEN    NON-NEG       0         0          0
 3    p3                 NON-NEG       0         0         -5.310497
 4    p4        BASIC    NON-NEG       0         1          0
 5    p5                 NON-NEG       0         0         -0.871045
 6    phi       BASIC    NON-NEG       1         1          0
 7    gain               SURPLUS       0         0         -0.013514
 8    cost               SLACK         0         0         -0.008066
 9    risk               SLACK         0         0         -0.241881
```

Figure 5.9 The output for the fourth DEA project analysis.

```
data deabook;
input _id_ $ p1 p2 p3 p4 p5 phi _type_ $ _rhs_;
cards;
obj 0 0 0 0 0 1 max .
gain 94 182 76 74 68 -68 ge 0
cost 20 95 66 64 12 0 le 12
risk 15 7 24 2 7 0 le 7
;
title 'project 5';
proc lp data=deabook;
run;
```

Figure 5.10 The code for the fifth DEA project analysis.

```
                    The LP Procedure
                    Variable Summary
       Variable                                              Reduced
Col    Name     Status   Type        Price   Activity         Cost
 1     p1                NON-NEG       0        0         -0.645085
 2     p2       DEGEN    NON-NEG       0        0                 0
 3     p3                NON-NEG       0        0            -2.813
 4     p4                NON-NEG       0        0         -0.420927
 5     p5       BASIC    NON-NEG       0        1                 0
 6     phi      BASIC    NON-NEG       1        1                 0
 7     gain              SURPLUS       0        0         -0.014706
 8     cost              SLACK         0        0         -0.020198
 9     risk              SLACK         0        0         -0.108231
```

Figure 5.11 The output for the fifth DEA project analysis.

Table 5.2 Summary of DEA efficiencies for the five projects.

Project	Efficiency	Reference project(s)
1	82.9%	Project 5
2	100.0%	None
3	28.4%	Projects 2 and 5
4	100.0%	None
5	100.0%	None

In this example, note that three of the projects are located on the efficient boundary and are all equally efficient at 100 percent. The project selection committee could use this DEA ranking information in several ways to guide its activities. The most direct way would be to fund projects with the highest efficiencies first. In this example this would mean that projects 2, 4, and 5 would have preference. But the committee also might take the view that inefficient projects should go back and review their assessments of the variables that keep them from achieving 100 percent efficiency. For example, if the slack is in the risk, perhaps actions to study and decrease this risk should be mandatory before funding is considered at all. Once the projects are all at 100 percent efficiency (or at least some minimum efficiency) then perhaps other selection mechanisms such as those presented in the other chapters of this book could be used to complete the selection of a funded Six Sigma project portfolio.

A REALISTIC DEA APPLICATION

In order to really demonstrate the power of the DEA technique, it is necessary to apply it to a more realistic example such as the 20-project and five-characteristic problems that have been discussed earlier. For this application, the cost will be considered as the single input that produces the four outputs of gain, risk, business objective, and training value. A linear programming problem has to be formulated and run for each of the 20 projects. Figure 5.12 shows the appropriate program code for project 18 alone and Figure 5.13 shows the associated output. Table 5.3 shows the efficiencies and the reference sets for the full set of 20 potential projects where each efficiency and reference project is computed by suitably modified versions of the same code.

EXTENSIONS OF THE DEA METHODS TO ENTIRE PORTFOLIOS

The discussion thus far in this chapter has treated each project as a separate entity in the DEA evaluation but this is not the only, nor probably the best, way in which to choose a Six Sigma project portfolio. One can also treat whole portfolios as the individual entities for the ranking and efficiency calculations performed as part of DEA. One can consider several portfolios of projects generated by another method perhaps or even all possible portfolios if the projects are not too numerous and the linear programming algorithm is efficient enough. To keep it simple here, only six project portfolios have been presented in previous examples out of the total of

```
data deabook;
input _id_ $ p1-p20 phi _type_ $ _rhs_;
cards;
obj 0 0 0 0 0 0 0 0 0 0 0 0 0 0 0 0 0 0 0 0 1 max .
gain 2 10 8 25 5 5 7 11 4 50 16 26 1 3 8 5 5 22 38 9 -22 ge 0
cost .3 .3 .2 5 1 .8 .2 .7 1 4 8 1.2 .2 .3 .8 .8 1.8 10 10 .9 0
le 10
risk 25 12 5 50 5 10 25 35 25 35 40 70 70 37 25 12 3 18 80 40 0
le 18
direct 1 2 2 1 3 3 2 1 1 3 1 1 3 1 1 2 1 2 1 1 0 le 2
cust 1 1 2 3 2 1 2 1 1 3 2 3 1 2 2 1 1 2 3 1 0 le 2
;
```

Figure 5.12 The DEA code for project 18.

```
                    The LP Procedure
                    Variable Summary
        Variable                                         Reduced
Col  Name     Status  Type        Price    Activity         Cost
  1  p1               NON-NEG         0           0    -1.482517
  2  p2               NON-NEG         0           0    -0.323427
  3  p3               NON-NEG         0           0    -0.02972
  4  p4               NON-NEG         0           0    -2.054196
  5  p5               NON-NEG         0           0    -0.166084
  6  p6               NON-NEG         0           0    -0.428322
  7  p7               NON-NEG         0           0    -1.298951
  8  p8               NON-NEG         0           0    -1.685315
  9  p9               NON-NEG         0           0    -1.391608
 10  p10      BASIC   NON-NEG         0   0.4615385            0
 11  p11              NON-NEG         0           0    -1.807692
 12  p12              NON-NEG         0           0    -3.232517
 13  p13              NON-NEG         0           0    -4.281469
 14  p14              NON-NEG         0           0    -2.215035
 15  p15              NON-NEG         0           0    -1.253497
 16  p16              NON-NEG         0           0    -0.550699
 17  p17      BASIC   NON-NEG         0   0.6153846            0
 18  p18              NON-NEG         0           0    -0.188811
 19  p19              NON-NEG         0           0    -3.298951
 20  p20              NON-NEG         0           0    -2.082168
 21  phi      BASIC   NON-NEG         1   1.1888112            0
 22  gain             SURPLUS         0           0    -0.045455
 23  cost     BASIC   SLACK           0   7.0461538            0
 24  risk             SLACK           0           0    -0.061189
 25  direct   DEGEN   SLACK           0           0            0
 26  cust             SLACK           0           0    -0.043706
```

Figure 5.13 The DEA output for project 18.

125 possible. Table 5.4 shows the total cost and total outputs for this representative set of these 125 possible portfolios. The same methodology using linear programming can now be applied using the full set of 125 as input/output pairs. Figure 5.14 shows the code that can be used to solve the appropriate linear programming problem for portfolio 5 in the list and Figure 5.15 shows the results. Table 5.5 shows the subsequent computation of efficiency for the entire set of two-project portfolios that can be generated in this simplified example.

If one accepts the efficiency estimates given in this table, then one could insist that the project characteristics be reworked so that they all become 100 percent efficient just as the portfolio consisting of projects J and L already is. For similar reasons the cost of the portfolios could be artificially lowered so in this way they become 100 percent efficient as well. One can

Table 5.3 The summary of DEA efficiencies and reference projects for 20 projects.

Project	Efficiency	Reference project(s)
1	84.2%	Projects 10 and 17
2	25.0%	Projects 2, 3, and 12
3	100.0%	None
4	91.8%	Projects 10, 12, and 19
5	61.8%	Projects 3 and 17
6	40.6%	Projects 2, 3, and 10
7	87.5%	Project 3
8	93.2%	Projects 2, 10, and 12
9	28.4%	Projects 2, 10, and 12
10	100.0%	None
11	18.4%	Projects 10 and 19
12	100.0%	None
13	42.9%	Projects 2 and 3
14	37.5%	Projects 3 and 12
15	55.9%	Projects 3, 10, and 12
16	37.8%	Projects 2 and 10
17	100.0%	None
18	84.2%	Projects 10 and 17
19	100.0%	None
20	67.5%	Projects 2, 10, and 12

Table 5.4 A subset of two-project portfolios.

Project name	Gain	Cost	Risk
J and K	15	1.7	60
J and L	61	4.7	60
J and M	27	8.7	75
K and L	54	5.0	60
K and M	20	9.0	65
L and M	66	12.0	75

58 Chapter Five

```
data deabook;
input _id_ $ p1-p6 phi _type_ $ _rhs_;
cards;
obj  0  0  0  0  0  0  1 max .
gain 14 61 27 54 20 66 -14 ge 0
cost 1.7 4.7 8.7 5.0 9.0 12.0  0 le 1.7
risk  60 60 75 60 65 75  0 le 60
;
title 'project portfolio JK';
proc lp data=deabook;
run;
```

Figure 5.14 The DEA code for the first project portfolio.

```
         Variable                                            Reduced
Col      Name      Status   Type         Price   Activity      Cost
  1      p1                 NON-NEG          0          0   -0.575988
  2      p2        BASIC    NON-NEG          0  0.3617021           0
  3      p3                 NON-NEG          0          0   -6.136778
  4      p4                 NON-NEG          0          0   -0.778116
  5      p5                 NON-NEG          0          0   -6.914894
  6      p6                 NON-NEG          0          0   -6.410334
  7      phi       BASIC    NON-NEG          1  1.5759878           0
  8      gain               SURPLUS          0          0   -0.071429
  9      cost               SLACK            0          0   -0.927052
 10      risk      BASIC    SLACK            0 38.297872           0
```

Figure 5.15 The DEA output for the first project portfolio.

Table 5.5 A summary of the DEA efficiencies and reference portfolios.

Portfolio	Efficiency	Reference portfolio(s)
Portfolio J and K	63.5%	Portfolio JL
Portfolio J and L	100.0%	None
Portfolio J and M	35.4%	Portfolio JL
Portfolio K and L	88.5%	Portfolio JL
Portfolio K and M	30.3%	Portfolio JL
Portfolio L and M	86.6%	Portfolio JL

also make good use of the efficient portfolio as a baseline for performance evaluation as presented in Chapter 8. There are many other refinements to DEA that could also be valuable for Six Sigma project portfolio selection that are discussed in the literature but not presented here.

RECIPE FOR THE METHOD USED IN THIS CHAPTER

Data Envelopment Method

Step 1 Run linear programming code for each project to find phi

Step 2 Convert phi to efficiency

Step 3 If efficiency equals 100 percent, then the project (portfolio) lies on the horizon and is a candidate for inclusion in the final portfolio

Step 4 (Optional) Alter characteristics of dominated projects (portfolios) until they too reach the horizon and can then be included in the final portfolio

6
Portfolio Selection Through Mathematical Programming

CONSTRAINTS VERSUS OBJECTIVES

Most of the methods that have been developed for the purposes of improving the Six Sigma project portfolio selection process thus far have treated the various characteristics of the projects as multiple characteristics or objectives. These characteristics could be anything in a real-world application but most often would include some terms related to the cost and the benefit of the project. Other common objectives in project selection may be related to risk, training targets, business directives, or customer requests. The standard selection method that is often recommended for Six Sigma usage is based on the ranking of individual projects based on these characteristics, with final funding decisions made by a management selection committee. It is left to the managers who make up this selection committee to make whatever trade-offs and compromises might be necessary to overcome the fundamental conflicts between the different objectives. This subjective method of combining the projects into a project portfolio can often be substantially outperformed by the more objective methods that are presented in this book. This book has introduced a number of methods such as MCDM, AHP, and DEA that can provide better ways of combining the projects, but all these methods still tend to view each project separately. They do not take full advantage of the benefits of a true portfolio approach to the selection process. Beginning with the present chapter and continuing through much of the remainder of the book, a true portfolio approach will be adopted. In order to accomplish this change of viewpoint, a new and powerful set of optimization tools called linear, integer, and nonlinear programming will be introduced and then used extensively. Specifically, this chapter will treat the use of linear programming for Six Sigma project portfolio selection, while Chapter 7 will do the same job for integer programming, and Chapter 10 will show the nonlinear method.

These programming methods offer some distinct advantages for Six Sigma project selection problems. They are well-developed methods that have been used in operations research and financial portfolio applications for decades. The thousands of real-world applications of these methods are responsible for billions of dollars in improved performance. They have become such an integral part of the optimization world that there are dozens of good software packages to support them, numerous training courses, and lots of experts to continue their development. There is no good reason why these methods should not be available to any Six Sigma practitioner who wants to use them. Some of the advantages of this linear programming approach are listed in Figure 6.1.

The fourth item in this list describes a feature that is very important to all optimization work but that has not been emphasized to this point. Sensitivity analyses allow the practitioner to study the impact caused by uncertainty in his assumptions on the optimal portfolio. Sensitivity analysis is such an integral part of almost all linear programming approaches that it will be included as a natural part of the development from this point onward. It will also be the subject of an entire later chapter as well. The other methods in this book, including the standard Six Sigma ranking method, do not allow one to easily study the sensitivity of the final solutions, and this can turn out to be a major deficiency of all of them in comparison to the mathematical programming methods.

- They have a distinct (usually unique) optimum
- They do not depend on weighting multiple objectives
- They focus attention on the financial aspects of Six Sigma
- They allow easy sensitivity analysis
- They allow access to a wide variety of theory and software
- They can handle problems of all sizes
- They can be solved more easily and more quickly
- They have been extensively used in financial portfolio construction

Figure 6.1 Some advantages of the linear programming approach.

LINEAR PROGRAMMING APPLICATION TO SIX SIGMA PROJECT PORTFOLIO SELECTION

To understand how linear programming can optimize a Six Sigma project portfolio it is useful to start the discussion with a simplified and slightly unrealistic form of the selection problem. Instead of considering the projects as all-or-nothing decisions, this chapter will take the viewpoint that they are more like financial instruments that can be invested at fractional levels that simply have to fall within some kind of budget cap or availability limit. Consider a simple two-project example similar to one that was introduced in an earlier chapter. Assume that there are two possible projects, A and B. Project A yields a return of $100K on every $20K invested for a 5 to 1 payoff rate. Project B yields a return of $80K on an investment of $10K for an 8 to 1 payoff rate. If the problem is to invest the entire $100K project funding budget in these two projects, then the problem of allocation is trivial. Since project B has a higher rate of return, simply put the full $100K into funding it for a benefit of ($80K/$10K) * $100K = $800K. Although it adds nothing fundamental in this simple problem, it is instructive to plot this relationship so that one can see how to handle more complicated situations.

One could plot this relationship as in Figure 6.2. Notice that this plot shows that putting all $100K into project A yields a $500K return and

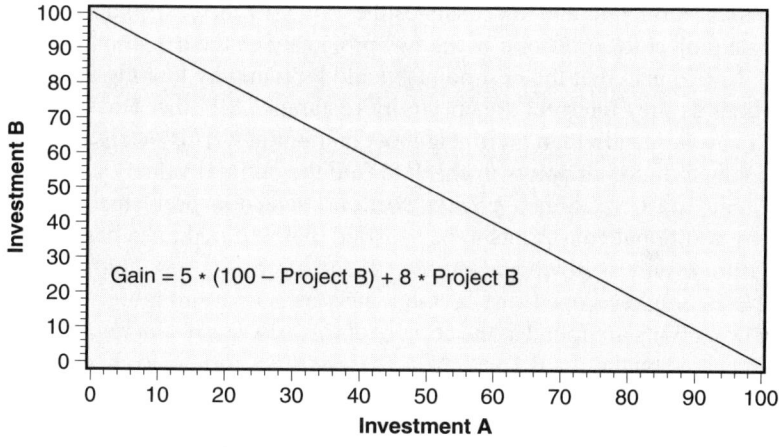

Figure 6.2 The two-project linear programming situation.

investing all $100K in project B yields an $800K return. Mixed investments yield returns that are intermediate to this lowest and highest achievable return. This relationship can be reduced to a single line given by the equation gain = 5 * (100 − amount invested in project B) + 8 * (amount invested in project B). Note that even though technically there are investments that are not on the line such as 20K in A and 20K in B, such portfolios are dominated by those mixes that are actually on the line. And notice further that one needs to check only the intersections of this line with the axes to find the two most likely candidate portfolios. One of these corner points is the best solution. It turns out that the types of problems for which linear programming is appropriate are those that have a single linear objective function and a set of linear constraints. For these situations there are efficient algorithms that identify the same small set of candidate points that were identified with the graphical approach. Furthermore, the algorithms automatically test each of these corner points until they arrive at an optimal solution, if one exists. This solution is mathematically guaranteed to be the best that is possible and no other portfolio can outperform it. In simple problems this best solution is usually obvious, but this is not the case for project selection problems with many possible projects and numerous complicated constraints. Regardless of these complications, the linear programming method eliminates any second-guessing that might occur after the solution portfolio is constructed.

Now consider the impact of imposing simple constraints on this problem. Assume that the maximum investment in project B is capped at $65K and project A is capped at $75K. The imposition of these constraints reduces the maximum gain and also changes the nature of the best solution from a single project to a portfolio of the two projects. See the depiction in Figure 6.3. Notice also that the best points would be found by looking at the tops of lines as they intersect the constraint rectangle. All other feasible points will have less gain than their neighbors on the lines. This means that there are now four corner points to check to find the optimal value.

But most Six Sigma project portfolio selection problems will have many additional constraints to be satisfied that will make the best-solution mixture even less obvious. Consider the addition of a new constraint that imposes another sloped line on the matrix as shown in Figure 6.4. Again the best points are found at the corners of this new constraint region, which is indicated by the shaded area. Now there are five corners to check but still this is remarkably less than might checked by a trial and error method on all combinations.

Each additional constraint will, in general, add another line to the figure. Constraints express restrictions on the investment relationships

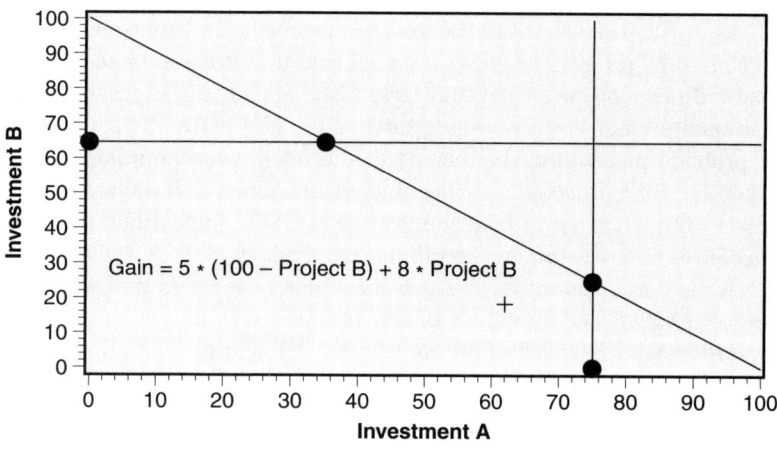

Figure 6.3 The two-project linear programming problem with constraints.

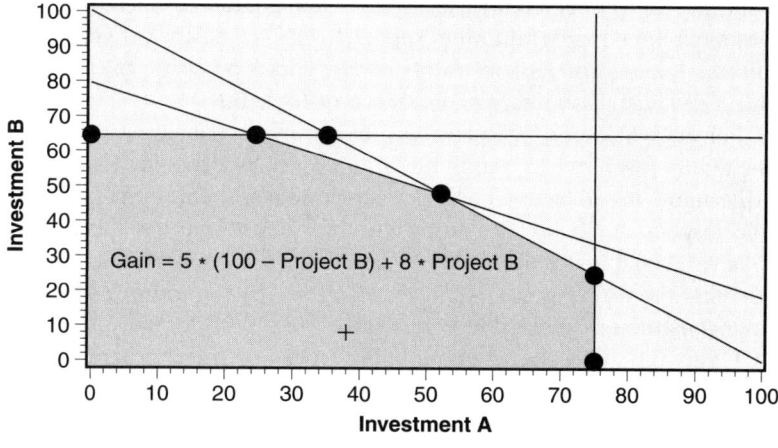

Figure 6.4 The two-project LP problem with two constraints.

between projects, and with 20 projects there would be a lot of possible constraints that might be active in a real problem. Although the graphics show that there is likely to be a rather easy search and identification approach based on the corner points of the appropriate region, this is still the type of problem that is best handled by a computer algorithm embedded in linear programming software.

As one can see based on the example problem, the extension from two projects to 20 projects would also complicate the situation in another way. A new dimension or axis would have to be added to the graph for each additional project over the original two. Now it is really difficult to solve the problem pictorially. One beauty of the linear programming approach is that the same procedure of checking corner points will produce the best answer even when the graphical depiction is all but impossible. Wonderful procedures like the simplex algorithm exist that can identify and efficiently search the corner points to arrive at the single best solution even for hundreds of projects and thousands of constraints.

The major drawback of the application of linear programming to project portfolio selection problems is the assumption that one may invest any amount in a project up to the maximum. Chapter 7 will show how the addition of further constraints can force the projects to be selected in an all-or-none process. But for now this chapter will stick with the less realistic situation in which fractional investments can be made. Often, simply rounding off the fractional values determined by the algorithm can lead to optimal integer portfolios, but this is not guaranteed. The fractional investment linear programming approach can be easily extended to 20 projects. And additional constraints can be added on costs, risks, training values, and business directives, as shown in Table 6.1.

For each of these projects it will be assumed that investment can be done at any level up to a maximum of the estimated cost for each project. Furthermore, it will be assumed that there are several important constraints to be respected. These are constraints that seek to ensure that a budget cap is respected and that a balance is maintained among funded projects with regard to their coverage of business directives and training objectives. These constraints are listed in Figure 6.5.

Figure 6.6 shows the SAS code using procedure linear programming in the operations research (OR) module that can solve this problem.

Finally, Figures 6.7 and 6.8 show the resulting best portfolio and its associated gain, cost, risk, training value, and customer value.

In this optimal Six Sigma project portfolio there is funding (at least partial funding) for projects 2, 3, 4, 5, 6, 10, 12, 15, 16, 17, and 18. The total gain is $2809K, which is achieved at a total cost of $400K and a total risk of 250. The number of projects that are aligned with business directive 1 is 3.0, 3.0 for directive 2, and 5.1 for directive 3. As for the training requirements, there are three Green Belt projects, 3.5 Black Belt projects, and 4.6 Master Black Belt projects. In the next chapter, the integer programming approach will provide a portfolio that allows only 'yes or no' funding of each project.

Table 6.1 A 20-project problem with multiple constraints.

Project name	Gain $100K	Cost $100K	% failure	Directive	Training
Project A	2	0.3	25	1	GB
Project C	10	0.3	12	2	GB
Project D	8	0.2	5	2, 3	BB
Project E	25	5.0	50	1, 2, 3	MBB
Project F	5	1.0	5	3	BB
Project G	5	0.8	10	3	GB
Project H	7	0.2	25	2	BB
Project J	11	0.7	35	1	GB
Project K	4	1.0	25	1	GB
Project L	50	4.0	35	3	MBB
Project M	16	8.0	40	1, 2	BB
Project N	26	1.2	70	1, 3	MBB
Project P	1	0.2	70	3	GB
Project Q	3	0.3	37	1	BB
Project R	8	0.8	25	1	BB
Project S	5	0.8	12	2	GB
Project T	5	1.8	3	1	GB
Project U	22	10.0	18	2, 3	BB
Project V	38	10.0	80	1, 2, 3	MBB
Project W	9	0.9	40	1, 3	BB

- Total cost less than or equal to $400K
- Total risk less than or equal to 450
- Number of directive 1 projects greater than or equal to three
- Number of directive 2 projects greater than or equal to three
- Number of directive 3 projects greater than or equal to three
- Number of Green Belt projects greater than or equal to three
- Number of Black Belt projects greater than or equal to three
- Number of Master Black Belt projects greater than or equal to three

Figure 6.5 A list of realistic Six Sigma project portfolio constraints.

```
data lpexamp;
input _id_ $ p1-p20 _type_ $ _rhs_;
cards;
gain    2 10 8 25 5 5 7 11 4 50 16 26 1 3 8 5 5 22 38 9  max  .
cost    .3 .3 .2 5 1 .8 .2 .7 1 4 8 1.2 .2 .3 .8 .8 1.8 10 10 .9  le  40
risk    25 12 5 50 5 10 25 35 25 35 40 70 70 37 25 12 3 18 80 40  le  250
direct1 1 0 0 1 0 0 0 1 1 0 1 1 0 1 1 0 1 0 1 1  ge  3
direct2 0 1 1 0 0 0 1 0 0 0 0 0 0 0 1 0 1 0 0 0  ge  3
direct3 0 0 0 0 1 1 0 0 0 1 0 0 1 0 0 0 0 0 0 0  ge  3
train1  1 1 0 0 0 1 0 1 1 0 0 0 1 0 0 1 1 0 0 1  ge  3
train2  0 0 1 0 1 0 1 0 0 0 1 0 0 1 1 0 0 1 0 0  ge  3
train3  0 0 0 1 0 0 0 0 0 1 0 1 0 0 0 0 0 0 1 0  ge  3
p1      1 0 0 0 0 0 0 0 0 0 0 0 0 0 0 0 0 0 0 0  le  .3
p2      0 1 0 0 0 0 0 0 0 0 0 0 0 0 0 0 0 0 0 0  le  .3
p3      0 0 1 0 0 0 0 0 0 0 0 0 0 0 0 0 0 0 0 0  le  .2
p4      0 0 0 1 0 0 0 0 0 0 0 0 0 0 0 0 0 0 0 0  le  5
p5      0 0 0 0 1 0 0 0 0 0 0 0 0 0 0 0 0 0 0 0  le  1
p6      0 0 0 0 0 1 0 0 0 0 0 0 0 0 0 0 0 0 0 0  le  .8
p7      0 0 0 0 0 0 1 0 0 0 0 0 0 0 0 0 0 0 0 0  le  .2
p8      0 0 0 0 0 0 0 1 0 0 0 0 0 0 0 0 0 0 0 0  le  .7
p9      0 0 0 0 0 0 0 0 1 0 0 0 0 0 0 0 0 0 0 0  le  1
p10     0 0 0 0 0 0 0 0 0 1 0 0 0 0 0 0 0 0 0 0  le  4
p11     0 0 0 0 0 0 0 0 0 0 1 0 0 0 0 0 0 0 0 0  le  8
p12     0 0 0 0 0 0 0 0 0 0 0 1 0 0 0 0 0 0 0 0  le  1.2
p13     0 0 0 0 0 0 0 0 0 0 0 0 1 0 0 0 0 0 0 0  le  .2
p14     0 0 0 0 0 0 0 0 0 0 0 0 0 1 0 0 0 0 0 0  le  .3
p15     0 0 0 0 0 0 0 0 0 0 0 0 0 0 1 0 0 0 0 0  le  .8
p16     0 0 0 0 0 0 0 0 0 0 0 0 0 0 0 1 0 0 0 0  le  .8
p17     0 0 0 0 0 0 0 0 0 0 0 0 0 0 0 0 1 0 0 0  le  1.8
p18     0 0 0 0 0 0 0 0 0 0 0 0 0 0 0 0 0 1 0 0  le  10
p19     0 0 0 0 0 0 0 0 0 0 0 0 0 0 0 0 0 0 1 0  le  10
p20     0 0 0 0 0 0 0 0 0 0 0 0 0 0 0 0 0 0 0 1  le  .9
;
title 'lp example';
proc lp data=lpexamp;
run;
```

Figure 6.6 The code for the realistic linear programming problem.

```
lp example
                        The LP Procedure
                        Variable Summary
         Variable                                              Reduced
    Col  Name      Status  Type        Price   Activity        Cost
      1  p1                NON-NEG        2          0      -4.868715
      2  p2        BASIC   NON-NEG       10        0.3              0
      3  p3        BASIC   NON-NEG        8        0.2              0
      4  p4        BASIC   NON-NEG       25   0.1856425             0
      5  p5        BASIC   NON-NEG        5          1              0
      6  p6        BASIC   NON-NEG        5        0.1              0
      7  p7                NON-NEG        7          0      -0.444693
      8  p8                NON-NEG       11          0      -0.416201
      9  p9                NON-NEG        4          0      -4.100559
     10  p10       BASIC   NON-NEG       50          4              0
     11  p11               NON-NEG       16          0     -10.43575
     12  p12       BASIC   NON-NEG       26   0.4257542             0
     13  p13               NON-NEG        1          0     -26.00559
     14  p14               NON-NEG        3          0      -8.732402
     15  p15       BASIC   NON-NEG        8   0.5886034             0
     16  p16       BASIC   NON-NEG        5        0.8              0
     17  p17       BASIC   NON-NEG        5        1.8              0
     18  p18       BASIC   NON-NEG       22        1.7              0
     19  p19               NON-NEG       38          0      -7.329609
     20  p20               NON-NEG        9          0      -4.689944
     21  cost              SLACK          0          0      -1.759777
     22  risk              SLACK          0          0      -0.384358
     23  direct1           SURPLUS        0          0      -3.01676
     24  direct2           SURPLUS        0          0      -2.516201
     25  direct3   BASIC   SURPLUS        0        2.1              0
     26  train1            SURPLUS        0          0      -0.251397
     27  train2    BASIC   SURPLUS        0   0.4886034             0
     28  train3    BASIC   SURPLUS        0   1.6113966             0
     29  p1        BASIC   SLACK          0        0.3              0
     30  p2                SLACK          0          0      -7.627374
     31  p3                SLACK          0          0      -8.242458
     32  p4        BASIC   SLACK          0   4.8143575             0
     33  p5                SLACK          0          0      -1.318436
     34  p6        BASIC   SLACK          0        0.7              0
     35  p7        BASIC   SLACK          0        0.2              0
     36  p8        BASIC   SLACK          0        0.7              0
     37  p9        BASIC   SLACK          0          1              0
     38  p10               SLACK          0          0     -29.50838
     39  p11       BASIC   SLACK          0          8              0
     40  p12       BASIC   SLACK          0   0.7742458             0
     41  p13       BASIC   SLACK          0        0.2              0
     42  p14       BASIC   SLACK          0        0.3              0
     43  p15       BASIC   SLACK          0   0.2113966             0
     44  p16               SLACK          0          0      -1.747486
     45  p17               SLACK          0          0      -3.947486
     46  p18       BASIC   SLACK          0        8.3              0
     47  p19       BASIC   SLACK          0         10              0
     48  p20       BASIC   SLACK          0        0.9              0
```

Figure 6.7 The output from the realistic linear programming problem.

```
lp example
                         The LP Procedure
                         Constraint Summary
        Constraint             S/S                           Dual
Row     Name       Type        Col       Rhs   Activity   Activity
   1    gain       OBJECTVE      .         0   280.9195       .
   2    cost       LE           21        40         40   1.7597765
   3    risk       LE           22       250        250   0.3843575
   4    direct1    GE           23         3          3  -3.01676
   5    direct2    GE           24         3          3  -2.516201
   6    direct3    GE           25         3        5.1          0
   7    train1     GE           26         3          3  -0.251397
   8    train2     GE           27         3  3.4886034          0
   9    train3     GE           28         3  4.6113966          0
  10    p1         LE           29       0.3          0          0
  11    p2         LE           30       0.3        0.3   7.6273743
  12    p3         LE           31       0.2        0.2   8.2424581
  13    p4         LE           32         5  0.1856425          0
  14    p5         LE           33         1          1   1.3184358
  15    p6         LE           34       0.8        0.1          0
  16    p7         LE           35       0.2          0          0
  17    p8         LE           36       0.7          0          0
  18    p9         LE           37         1          0          0
  19    p10        LE           38         4          4  29.50838
  20    p11        LE           39         8          0          0
  21    p12        LE           40       1.2  0.4257542          0
  22    p13        LE           41       0.2          0          0
  23    p14        LE           42       0.3          0          0
  24    p15        LE           43       0.8  0.5886034          0
  25    p16        LE           44       0.8        0.8   1.747486
  26    p17        LE           45       1.8        1.8   3.947486
  27    p18        LE           46        10        1.7          0
  28    p19        LE           47        10          0          0
  29    p20        LE           48       0.9          0          0
```

Figure 6.8 The constraint part of the output for the realistic linear programming problem.

SENSITIVITY ANALYSIS

The solutions that are generated by linear programming for investment choices or Six Sigma project portfolio choices are guaranteed to be optimal if the data and assumptions that are used in the construction of the constraints and the objective function are correct. In most practical situations, including Six Sigma project selection, there is some uncertainty in this data. For example, the constraints in the example problem above might be $400K nominally but possibly could be stretched if there was a significant jump in the expected gains. Even the qualitative nature of the solution may change if the numbers in the constraints change dramatically. The methodology of linear programming makes it easy to examine the sensitivity of the solution to changes in the values used to characterize the problem (Hiller and Lieberman 1974).

As an example, one can consider the sensitivity of the simple situation given above. A possible question that sensitivity analysis of this problem might answer is, What effect does the changing of the constraint values have on the overall gain and on the structure of the portfolio itself? Another interesting question might be, What is the impact of changing the expected gains for some of the factors? It is these kinds of questions and more that sensitivity analysis can examine.

Let us consider three particular questions about the 20-project portfolio selection problem described above. First, consider the impact of an increase in the cost of several of the riskier projects. For definiteness assume that the cost of project M is underestimated by $200K so that it actually will cost $1 million dollars. Running the program code given in Figure 6.9 (after the original code is run) yields the sensitivity analysis given in Figure 6.10. Other options for sensitivity analysis include parametric programming.

```
proc lp data=lpexamp rangeprice primalout=solution;
run;
data sen;
input _id_ $ p1-p20 _type_ $ _rhs_;
cards;
pricesen 0 0 0 0 0 0 0 0 0 1 0 0 0 0 0 0 0 0 0 0 pricesen 2
;
data; set lpexamp sen;
proc lp primalin=solution;
run;
```

Figure 6.9 The code for sensitivity of price.

lp example

The LP Procedure
Price Range Analysis

```
         Variable--------Minimum Phi------- --------Maximum Phi-------
Col  Name        Price Entering     Objective  Price Entering   Objective
  1  p1          -INFINITY .           280.9195 6.8687151 p1      280.9195
  2  p2           2.3726257 p2         278.63128 INFINITY .        INFINITY
  3  p3          -0.242458 p3          279.27101 INFINITY .        INFINITY
  4  p4          24.29486 p16          280.78859 25.17936 p7       280.95279
  5  p5           3.6815642 p5         279.60106 INFINITY .        INFINITY
  6  p6           4.5837989 p8         280.87788 5.2513966 train1  280.94464
  7  p7          -INFINITY .           280.9195 7.4446927 p7       280.9195
  8  p8          -INFINITY .           280.9195 11.416201 p8       280.9195
  9  p9          -INFINITY .           280.9195 8.1005587 p9       280.9195
 10  p10         20.49162 p10          162.88598 INFINITY .        INFINITY
 11  p11         -INFINITY .           280.9195 26.435754 p11      280.9195
 12  p12         25.709913 p7          280.79599 27.71116 p16      281.64803
 13  p13         -INFINITY .           280.9195 27.005587 p13      280.9195
 14  p14         -INFINITY .           280.9195 11.732402 p14      280.9195
 15  p15          7.6218274 p8         280.6969 8.8333333 train1   281.41
 16  p16          3.252514 p16         279.52151 INFINITY .        INFINITY
 17  p17          1.052514 p17         273.81402 INFINITY .        INFINITY
 18  p18         21.555307 p7          280.16352 23.747486 p16     283.89022
 19  p19         -INFINITY .           280.9195 45.329609 p19      280.9195
 20  p20         -INFINITY .           280.9195 13.689944 p20      280.9195
 21  cost        -INFINITY .           280.9195 1.7597765 cost     280.9195
 22  risk        -INFINITY .           280.9195 0.3843575 risk     280.9195
 23  direct1     -INFINITY .           280.9195 3.0167598 direct1  280.9195
 24  direct2     -INFINITY .           280.9195 2.5162011 direct2  280.9195
 25  direct3     -0.416201 p8          280.04547 0.2513966 train1  281.44743
 26  train1      -INFINITY .           280.9195 0.2513966 train1   280.9195
 27  train2      -0.378173 p8          280.73472 0.7112324 p16     281.26701
 28  train3      -0.833333 train1      279.57667 0.4698937 p7      281.67668
 29  p1          -4.868715 p1          279.45888 INFINITY .        INFINITY
 30  p2          -INFINITY .           280.9195 7.6273743 p2       280.9195
 31  p3          -INFINITY .           280.9195 8.2424581 p3       280.9195
 32  p4          -0.17936 p7           280.05599 0.7051398 p16     284.31429
 33  p5          -INFINITY .           280.9195 1.3184358 p5       280.9195
 34  p6          -0.251397 train1      280.74352 0.4162011 p8      281.21084
 35  p7          -0.444693 p7          280.83056 INFINITY .        INFINITY
 36  p8          -0.416201 p8          280.62816 INFINITY .        INFINITY
 37  p9          -4.100559 p9          276.81894 INFINITY .        INFINITY
 38  p10         -INFINITY .           280.9195 29.50838 p10       280.9195
 39  p11         -10.43575 p11         197.43346 INFINITY .        INFINITY
 40  p12         -1.71116 p16          279.59464 0.2900875 p7      281.1441
 41  p13         -26.00559 p13         275.71838 INFINITY .        INFINITY
 42  p14         -8.732402 p14         278.29978 INFINITY .        INFINITY
 43  p15         -0.833333 train1      280.74333 0.3781726 p8      280.99944
 44  p16         -INFINITY .           280.9195 1.747486 p16       280.9195
 45  p17         -INFINITY .           280.9195 3.947486 p17       280.9195
 46  p18         -1.747486 p16         266.41536 0.4446927 p7      284.61045
 47  p19         -7.329609 p19         207.62341 INFINITY .        INFINITY
 48  p20         -4.689944 p20         276.69855 INFINITY .        INFINITY
```

Figure 6.10 The output for sensitivity of price.

RECIPE FOR THE METHOD USED IN THIS CHAPTER

Linear Programming Method

Step 1 Create linear objective function

Step 2 Create linear constraints

Step 3 Solve the allocation through linear programming

Step 4 If need be, round off the non-integer values

Step 5 (Optional but recommended) Perform sensitivity analyses

7
Six Sigma Project Portfolio Selection Through Integer Programming

THE NEED FOR INTEGER PROGRAMMING

The methods presented in Chapter 6 are guaranteed to provide the best solution to the problem of selecting a Six Sigma project portfolio while respecting the various sets of constraints that have been established, if partial funding is allowed. These methods are easily implemented by using any of the many good algorithms and software packages that are available. In addition to the ability to produce the optimal answers, linear programming methods also make it easy to conduct sensitivity analyses and other operations like goal programming.

But, as valuable as these linear programming approaches are for guiding the selection of project portfolios, they do have one limitation that detracts from their value. This weakness stems from the fact that they require the assumption that each project can be funded in fractional amounts of any degree. This was illustrated in Chapter 6 where some of the examples were assigned funding that was not 'all or none' as it would normally be in real-world scenarios. Sometimes the linear programming method will automatically produce all-integer project funding but this is not guaranteed in the most general situations. This assumption is perfectly fine for many financial and resource allocation problems, but most projects must be funded on an all or none basis, that is, their coefficients must be constrained to be zero or one instead of decimal values.

As an example of what this integer constraint means, one can reconsider the simple two-project portfolio example that has been used in previous chapters. In this example there are two projects, A and B. Project A provides a gain of $100K on a cost of $20K and project B promises $80K on a $10K investment. If there are no budget constraints, then this problem is trivial even with integer constraints since one would simply fund both projects fully at total cost of $30K for an expected gain of $180K. But if there is a cost constraint that the total budget is only $25K, then the problem is harder although still rather trivial in this case because of the simplicity of the example. With this cost constraint active, the linear programming solution without any restriction is to fully fund project B and fund project A at 70 percent. This should yield $80 + .75 * 100K = $155K at a cost of $20K + $5K = $25K. This is the best that one can do in this case. For example, funding all of project A and .50 of project B costs $25K but only yields $100K + $50K = $150K. In either case, all the available budget can be used to fund projects.

If one now adds the additional constraint that the projects must be funded completely or not at all then the solution changes. In this simple example one can see the correct answer simply by complete enumeration of the possibilities. One option is to completely fund project A, but this will not leave enough to fund project B. In this scenario the gain will be $100K for an outlay of $20K and there will be $5K of leftover funds. The other possibility is to fund all of project B but not project A. But this possibility costs $10K and earns only $80K. So the funding of project A is the clear winner. Notice that in each solution the gain is less than that achievable with the unconstrained linear programming solution. This will be true in general for all the integer-constrained problems no matter what their complexity may be.

Based on this example it appears that it should not be too difficult to apply integer programming (SAS 1989) to get a more realistic answer to the all-or-nothing funding assumed to be the case in Six Sigma project funding. Through examination of the given SAS code it should be possible for the reader to translate the problem into whatever integer programming software is available. While modern software makes this statement almost true there is some difficulty hidden beneath the apparent simplicity when it comes to integer problems. For one thing, the algorithms have to become more complicated than the simplex method that is commonly applied to the linear problem. One of the most common integer programming algorithms is based on the branch-and-bound approach (SAS 1989). This method is much less efficient than the pure linear programming algorithm but there is almost no discernable difference for any but very large problems if one has a good set of efficient code.

To understand the workings of the integer programming method, consider the simple problem given for the two projects above. This problem is small enough to be solved by simple complete enumeration but it will serve as a simple example of how an efficient search can be done in more complicated situations. Branch-and-bound operates by sequencing a series of linear programming problems in such a way that one can be assured of reaching the optimal integer solution. This branch-and-bound approach works in a series of steps. Step one in each iteration is to relax the integer constraints and simply solve the equivalent linear programming problem. Step two is to create new subproblems based on the results from step 1 by adding constraints on one new variable. By working these iterations it is possible to eventually branch through all the options and arrive at an optimal solution, always assuming that any such solution is possible.

The details of the branch-and-bound method can be illustrated for the simple problem. In this case the first step is to ignore the integer constraints and simply solve this problem for the optimal-gain Six Sigma project portfolio. Figure 7.1 shows the code for this subproblem. The solution calls for a fractional investment in project A of 0.75, as we have seen above. Since this is not an integer then it is not feasible for the actual problem and more searching needs to be performed. If the weights are all integers then the solution is feasible and one can stop here knowing that the best integer solution has been found. The branch-and-bound algorithm now takes one of the projects that has a fractional weight and creates two new optimization problems from it by modifying or adding a constraint from the original problem formulation. In this example only project A has a fractional value, so it is the only candidate. These results are shown in Figure 7.2.

```
data simple;
input _id_ $ p1 p2 _type_ $ _rhs_;
cards;
benefit 100 80 max .
cost 20 10 le 25
available 1 1 upperbd .
available 0 0 lowerbd .
;
proc lp data=simple; run;
```

Figure 7.1 The code for the first branch-and-bound step.

```
                    Variable Summary
       Variable                                          Reduced
Col    Name      Status  Type       Price   Activity      Cost
  1    p1        BASIC   UPLOWBD     100      0.75          0
  2    p2        UPPBD   UPLOWBD      80      1            30
  3    cost              SLACK         0      0            -5

                    Constraint Summary
       Constraint           S/S                         Dual
Row    Name      Type       Col      Rhs   Activity    Activity
  1    benefit   OBJECTVE    .         0    155            .
  2    cost      LE          3        25     25            5
```

Figure 7.2 The output for the first branch-and-bound step.

The two new problems are identical to the old ones in that they keep all the original constraints except that now a new constraint is added. The first problem now includes the constraint that project A investment must be greater than or equal to 1. The best solution to this problem is to spend $20K on project 1 and $5K on project 2 for a total gain of $140K. But this still has a non-integer weight so now two more subproblems are created, one with the constraint that project A funding is ≥ 1 and project B funding is ≥ 1. But this problem has no solution since there is not enough money to fully fund both projects, so this is a dead end. The other new subproblem has the constraints of project A funding ≥ 1 and project funding for B ≤ 0. The solution here is to fund only project A for a cost of $20K and a gain of $100K. Returning to the other half of the initial subproblem, the constraints are imposed that the funding for project A ≤ 0, which leads to the solution that project B is fully funded only. This branch solution has a gain of $80K, which is less than the $100K that is possible with just the opposite funding pattern. Having exhausted all the possible branches, the final integer-constrained portfolio solution is to completely fund project A and to neglect project B for a gain of $100K. The branch-and-bound approach uses the efficient linear programming solution methods coupled with a clever search technique to isolate the final optimal integer solution. Figure 7.3 summarizes this branch-and-bound integer programming approach.

There are many other integer programming techniques that are available if needed for larger and more complex problems, but for most Six Sigma project portfolio selection problems this branch-and-bound approach should be sufficient.

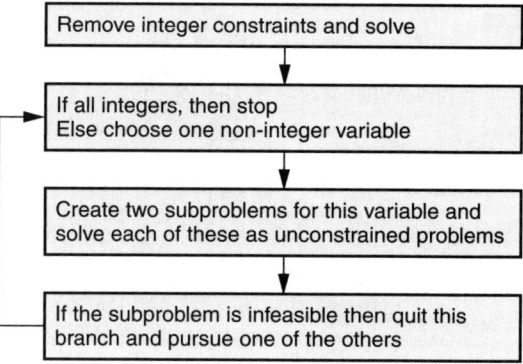

Figure 7.3 The simple branch-and-bound logic.

```
data lpexamp;
input _id_ $ p1-p20 _type_ $ _rhs_;
cards;
gain 2 10 8 25 5 5 7 11 4 50 16 26 1 3 8 5 5 22 38 9 max .
cost .3 .3 .2 5 1 .8 .2 .7 1 4 8 1.2 .2 .3 .8 .8 1.8 10 10 .9 le
40
risk 25 12 5 50 5 10 25 35 25 35 40 70 70 37 25 12 3 18 80 40 le
250
available 1 1 1 1 1 1 1 1 1 1 1 1 1 1 1 1 1 1 1 1 upperbd .
available 0 0 0 0 0 0 0 0 0 0 0 0 0 0 0 0 0 0 0 0 lowerbd .
integer   1 1 1 1 1 1 1 1 1 1 1 1 1 1 1 1 1 1 1 1 integer .
;
title 'lp example';
proc lp data=lpexamp;
run;
```

Figure 7.4 The 20-project integer programming code.

A MORE REALISTIC INTEGER PROGRAMMING PROBLEM

Of course problems like the simple one above are not typical of real Six Sigma project portfolio selection applications. In order to better see the differences between linear and integer programming it will be necessary to consider a more realistic problem such as that of the 20 projects with the cost and risk constraints. Figure 7.4 shows the SAS code that solves

```
                    Variable Summary
      Variable                                    Reduced
  Col Name      Status Type       Price  Activity  Cost
    1 p1               BINARY        2       0        2
    2 p2               BINARY       10       1       10
    3 p3               BINARY        8       1        8
    4 p4               BINARY       25       1       25
    5 p5               BINARY        5       1        5
    6 p6               BINARY        5       0        5
    7 p7               BINARY        7       0        7
    8 p8               BINARY       11       0       11
    9 p9               BINARY        4       0        4
   10 p10              BINARY       50       1       50
   11 p11              BINARY       16       0       16
   12 p12              BINARY       26       0       26
   13 p13              BINARY        1       0        1
   14 p14              BINARY        3       0        3
   15 p15              BINARY        8       1        8
   16 p16              BINARY        5       1        5
   17 p17              BINARY        5       1        5
   18 p18              BINARY       22       1       22
   19 p19              BINARY       38       1       38
   20 p20              BINARY        9       0        9
   21 cost      BASIC  SLACK         0      6.1       0
   22 risk      BASIC  SLACK         0       5        0

  int example
                        The LP Procedure
                       Constraint Summary

       Constraint         S/S                        Dual
  Row  Name      Type     Col    Rhs  Activity  Activity
    1  gain     OBJECTVE    .      0     176         .
    2  cost     LE         21     40    33.9         0
    3  risk     LE         22    250    245          0
```

Figure 7.5 The output for the 20-project integer programming problem.

the same 20-project problem with the additional integer constraints on the funding of each project. Figure 7.5 then shows the output produced by executing this code.

Figure 7.6 compares the linear programming solution with this integer programming solution to show that they are not completely interconvertible. Notice that, in general, the addition of extra constraints such as the integer constraints makes the problem harder to solve and hence produces a lower expected gain.

Among other differences between the two methods one can observe that the estimated gain for the integer-constrained problem is $1810K –

```
                      Variable Summary
      Variable                                          Reduced
Col   Name      Status  Type        Price   Activity    Cost

  1   p1                UPLOWBD       2        0         -8
  2   p2        UPPBD   UPLOWBD      10        1          5.2
  3   p3        UPPBD   UPLOWBD       8        1          6
  4   p4        UPPBD   UPLOWBD      25        1          5
  5   p5        UPPBD   UPLOWBD       5        1          3
  6   p6        UPPBD   UPLOWBD       5        1          1
  7   p7                UPLOWBD       7        0         -3
  8   p8                UPLOWBD      11        0         -3
  9   p9                UPLOWBD       4        0         -6
 10   p10       UPPBD   UPLOWBD      50        1         36
 11   p11       BASIC   UPLOWBD      16        0.5        0
 12   p12               UPLOWBD      26        0         -2
 13   p13               UPLOWBD       1        0        -27
 14   p14               UPLOWBD       3        0        -11.8
 15   p15               UPLOWBD       8        0         -2
 16   p16       UPPBD   UPLOWBD       5        1          0.2
 17   p17       UPPBD   UPLOWBD       5        1          3.8
 18   p18       UPPBD   UPLOWBD      22        1         14.8
 19   p19       UPPBD   UPLOWBD      38        1          6
 20   p20               UPLOWBD       9        0         -7
 21   cost      BASIC   SLACK         0        2.1        0
 22   risk              SLACK         0        0         -0.4

1pt example
                        The LP Procedure
                       Constraint Summary

      Constraint             S/S                       Dual
Row   Name      Type         Col      Rhs   Activity   Activity

  1   gain      OBJECTVE      .         0      181         .
  2   cost      LE           21        40       37.9       0
  3   risk      LE           22       250      250         0.4
```

Figure 7.6 The output for the 20-project problem using linear programming.

$1760K = $50K less, the costs are different, and project 11 is funded at a fractional level in the nonconstrained solution. Perhaps most telling is the fact that the actual funded portfolios are different.

ADDING MORE CONSTRAINTS

To increase the complexity and practicality of the problems, one can add additional constraints that target minimum requirements for business

```
data intexamp;
input _id_ $ p1-p20 _type_ $ _rhs_;
cards;
gain  2 10 8 25 5 5 7 11 4 50 16 26 1 3 8 5 5 22 38 9 max .
cost .3 .3 .2 5 1 .8 .2 .7 1 4 8 1.2 .2 .3 .8 .8 1.8 10 10 .9 le 40
risk 25 12 5 50 5 10 25 35 25 35 40 70 70 37 25 12 3 18 80 40 le 250
direct1 1 0 0 1 0 0 0 1 1 0 1 1 0 1 1 0 1 0 1 1 ge 3
direct2 0 1 1 0 0 0 1 0 0 0 0 0 0 0 1 0 1 0 0 ge 3
direct3 0 0 0 0 1 1 0 0 0 1 0 0 1 0 0 0 0 0 0 0 ge 3
train1  1 1 0 0 0 1 0 1 1 0 0 0 1 0 0 1 1 0 0 1 ge 3
train2  0 0 1 0 1 0 1 0 0 0 1 0 0 1 1 0 0 1 0 0 ge 3
train3  0 0 0 1 0 0 0 0 0 1 0 1 0 0 0 0 0 0 1 0 ge 3
available 1 1 1 1 1 1 1 1 1 1 1 1 1 1 1 1 1 1 1 1 upperbd .
available 0 0 0 0 0 0 0 0 0 0 0 0 0 0 0 0 0 0 0 0 lowerbd .
integer   1 1 1 1 1 1 1 1 1 1 1 1 1 1 1 1 1 1 1 1 integer .
;
title 'integer example';
proc lp data=lpexamp;
run;
```

Figure 7.7 Integer code for the 20-project problem with more constraints.

directive coverage and training value in addition to the previous constraints on cost and risk. This is the list of projects already given as Table 4.1. Again, the introduction of more constraints will in general make the gains less than those for unconstrained problems. And the addition of integer constraints just makes it harder to achieve the full potential of the unconstrained problem. Figure 7.7 shows the integer programming code and Figure 7.8 the integer solution portfolio.

For ease of comparison, the results obtained for this problem using linear programming without integer constraints is repeated in Figure 7.9.

There are many differences in the two answers, with the most notable being the existence of partially funded projects and hence nonidentical portfolios. Remember however that in each case the solution portfolio is optimal and cannot be bettered, assuming the correctness of the inputs. The difference between the solutions is entirely due to the extra integer constraints on the project funding. Generally, the addition of these extra constraints makes it harder to find a solution and, once that solution is found, it can be no better than the unconstrained solution.

Six Sigma Project Portfolio Selection Through Integer Programming 83

```
                         Variable Summary
         Variable                                        Reduced
    Col  Name      Status  Type       Price  Activity    Cost
     1   p1                BINARY       2       0          2
     2   p2                BINARY      10       1         10
     3   p3                BINARY       8       1          8
     4   p4                BINARY      25       1         25
     5   p5                BINARY       5       1          5
     6   p6                BINARY       5       1          5
     7   p7                BINARY       7       0          7
     8   p8                BINARY      11       0         11
     9   p9                BINARY       4       0          4
    10   p10               BINARY      50       1         50
    11   p11               BINARY      16       0         16
    12   p12               BINARY      26       0         26
    13   p13               BINARY       1       0          1
    14   p14               BINARY       3       0          3
    15   p15               BINARY       8       1          8
    16   p16               BINARY       5       0          5
    17   p17               BINARY       5       1          5
    18   p18               BINARY      22       1         22
    19   p19               BINARY      38       1         38
    20   p20               BINARY       9       0          9
    21   cost      BASIC   SLACK        0       6.1        0
    22   risk      BASIC   SLACK        0       7          0
    23   direct1   BASIC   SURPLUS      0       1          0
    24   direct2   DEGEN   SURPLUS      0       0          0
    25   direct3   DEGEN   SURPLUS      0       0          0
    26   train1    DEGEN   SURPLUS      0       0          0
    27   train2    BASIC   SURPLUS      0       1          0
    28   train3    DEGEN   SURPLUS      0       0          0
integer example
                           The LP Procedure
                           Constraint Summary
         Constraint         S/S                          Dual
    Row  Name      Type     Col    Rhs   Activity    Activity
     1   gain      OBJECTVE   .      0      176           .
     2   cost      LE        21     40       33.9         0
     3   risk      LE        22    250      243           0
     4   direct1   GE        23      3        4           0
     5   direct2   GE        24      3        3           0
     6   direct3   GE        25      3        3           0
     7   train1    GE        26      3        3           0
     8   train2    GE        27      3        4           0
     9   train3    GE        28      3        3           0
```

Figure 7.8 Solution to the 20-project problem with more constraints.

```
                    Variable Summary
        Variable                                        Reduced
Col  Name        Status   Type      Price   Activity   Cost
  1  p1                   UPLOWBD      2       0         -8
  2  p2          UPPBD    UPLOWBD     10       1          5.2
  3  p3          UPPBD    UPLOWBD      8       1          6
  4  p4          UPPBD    UPLOWBD     25       1          5
  5  p5          UPPBD    UPLOWBD      5       1          3
  6  p6          UPPBD    UPLOWBD      5       1          1
  7  p7                   UPLOWBD      7       0         -3
  8  p8                   UPLOWBD     11       0         -3
  9  p9                   UPLOWBD      4       0         -6
 10  p10         UPPBD    UPLOWBD     50       1         36
 11  p11         BASIC    UPLOWBD     16       0.5        0
 12  p12                  UPLOWBD     26       0         -2
 13  p13                  UPLOWBD      1       0        -27
 14  p14                  UPLOWBD      3       0        -11.8
 15  p15                  UPLOWBD      8       0         -2
 16  p16         UPPBD    UPLOWBD      5       1          0.2
 17  p17         UPPBD    UPLOWBD      5       1          3.8
 18  p18         UPPBD    UPLOWBD     22       1         14.8
 19  p19         UPPBD    UPLOWBD     38       1          6
 20  p20                  UPLOWBD      9       0         -7
 21  cost        BASIC    SLACK        0       2.1        0
 22  risk                 SLACK        0       0         -0.4
 23  direct1     BASIC    SURPLUS      0       0.5        0
 24  direct2     BASIC    SURPLUS      0       1          0
 25  direct3     DEGEN    SURPLUS      0       0          0
 26  train1      BASIC    SURPLUS      0       1          0
 27  train2      BASIC    SURPLUS      0       0.5        0
 28  train3      DEGEN    SURPLUS      0       0          0
integer example
                       The LP Procedure
                       Constraint Summary
       Constraint          S/S                            Dual
Row  Name      Type        Col     Rhs   Activity      Activity
  1  gain      OBJECTVE      .       0     181            .
  2  cost      LE           21      40      37.9          0
  3  risk      LE           22     250     250            0.4
  4  direct1   GE           23       3       3.5          0
  5  direct2   GE           24       3       4            0
  6  direct3   GE           25       3       3            0
  7  train1    GE           26       3       4            0
  8  train2    GE           27       3       3.5          0
  9  train3    GE           28       3       3            0
```

Figure 7.9 The linear programming solution to the 20-project problem with full constraints.

SENSITIVITY ANALYSIS FOR INTEGER PROGRAMMING

Even though the nature of integer constraints on the selection of project portfolios makes the solution harder to produce it is still vital to be able to perform appropriate sensitivity analysis. It is only through sensitivity analysis that one can understand the limitations that are placed like quotation marks around the optimal solution that the programming methods produce. The optimality depends on one's knowledge of the values that go into the problem formulation. It is important in real applications to appreciate that the optimal solution depends on the particular coefficients that one inserts into the problem.

Sensitivity analysis is almost unnecessary to perform in the case of linear programming methods. It is not as easy to do a full sensitivity analysis in the case of an integer-constrained Six Sigma project portfolio selection but it is still important to do it nevertheless. Probably the simplest way to do the sensitivity analysis is to change some of the values in the problem and then simply rerun the problem and obtain a new solution. In some cases the solution will involve the same portfolio of projects but with altered gains, costs, risks, and other characteristics. This is interesting but usually not critical to the actual selection process. However, some changes will cause a change in the portfolio itself with different projects being identified. This is more interesting in practical applications since it implies a significant change in strategy. Assuming that one has efficient code and a reasonably sized problem, these what-if reruns of the integer program should not make the process unduly difficult. In most applications it is the number of what-if questions that causes the most difficulty rather than the length of time necessary to rerun the solution of any one of them.

For example, one might want to see if the solution changes if there is doubt about the cost of project 2 of the 20-project portfolio example. Perhaps there was an oversight by the project team that left out a step and the real cost should be $0.8K rather than the original $0.3K. Management would like to see how this change could affect the original portfolio already identified above with the full set of constraints on business direction and training value. Figure 7.10 shows the detailed code for this integer programming sensitivity analysis and Figure 7.11 shows the associated output.

In this case the optimal Six Sigma project portfolio is still the same. Indeed, all characteristics stay the same for the new portfolio except the total cost, which is now $34.4K rather than the original $33.9K, which is the difference of $0.5K that is entirely reflected in the projected increased cost of project 2.

```
data intsens1;
input _id_ $ p1-p20 _type_ $ _rhs_;
cards;
gain 2 10 8 25 5 5 7 11 4 50 16 26 1 3 8 5 5 22 38 9 max .
cost .3 .8 .2 5 1 .8 .2 .7 1 4 8 1.2 .2 .3 .8 .8 1.8 10 10 .9 le
40
risk 25 12 5 50 5 10 25 35 25 35 40 70 70 37 25 12 3 18 80 40 le
250
direct1  1 0 0 1 0 0 0 1 1 0 1 1 0 1 1 0 1 0 1 1 ge 3
direct2  0 1 1 0 0 0 1 0 0 0 0 0 0 0 1 0 1 0 0 0 ge 3
direct3  0 0 0 0 1 1 0 0 0 1 0 0 1 0 0 0 0 0 0 0 ge 3
train1   1 1 0 0 0 1 0 1 1 0 0 0 1 0 0 1 1 0 0 1 ge 3
train2   0 0 1 0 1 0 1 0 0 0 1 0 0 1 1 0 0 1 0 0 ge 3
train3   0 0 0 1 0 0 0 0 0 1 0 1 0 0 0 0 0 0 1 0 ge 3
available 1 1 1 1 1 1 1 1 1 1 1 1 1 1 1 1 1 1 1 1 upperbd .
available 0 0 0 0 0 0 0 0 0 0 0 0 0 0 0 0 0 0 0 0 lowerbd .
integer   1 1 1 1 1 1 1 1 1 1 1 1 1 1 1 1 1 1 1 1 integer .
;
title 'integer sensitivity 1 example';
proc lp data=intsens1;
run;
```

Figure 7.10 Code for sensitivity analysis #1.

```
                     Variable Summary
       Variable                                   Reduced
Col    Name    Status  Type       Price  Activity  Cost

  1  p1               BINARY        2       0        2
  2  p2               BINARY       10       1       10
  3  p3               BINARY        8       1        8
  4  p4               BINARY       25       1       25
  5  p5               BINARY        5       1        5
  6  p6               BINARY        5       1        5
  7  p7               BINARY        7       0        7
  8  p8               BINARY       11       0       11
  9  p9               BINARY        4       0        4
 10  p10              BINARY       50       1       50
 11  p11              BINARY       16       0       16
 12  p12              BINARY       26       0       26
 13  p13              BINARY        1       0        1
 14  p14              BINARY        3       0        3
 15  p15              BINARY        8       1        8
 16  p16              BINARY        5       0        5
 17  p17              BINARY        5       1        5
 18  p18              BINARY       22       1       22
 19  p19              BINARY       38       1       38
 20  p20              BINARY        9       0        9
 21  cost    BASIC   SLACK         0      5.6       0
 22  risk    BASIC   SLACK         0       7        0
```

Figure 7.11 Results of the integer sensitivity analysis run #1.

```
                    Variable Summary
       Variable                                       Reduced
  Col  Name     Status  Type       Price  Activity    Cost
   23  direct1  BASIC   SURPLUS      0      1           0
   24  direct2  DEGEN   SURPLUS      0      0           0
   25  direct3  DEGEN   SURPLUS      0      0           0
   26  train1   DEGEN   SURPLUS      0      0           0
   27  train2   BASIC   SURPLUS      0      1           0
   28  train3   DEGEN   SURPLUS      0      0           0

integer sensitivity 1 example
                         The LP Procedure
                        Constraint Summary
      Constraint             S/S                         Dual
  Row  Name    Type          Col    Rhs  Activity      Activity
   1   gain    OBJECTVE       .      0     176            .
   2   cost    LE            21     40      34.4          0
   3   risk    LE            22    250     243            0
   4   direct1 GE            23      3       4            0
   5   direct2 GE            24      3       3            0
   6   direct3 GE            25      3       3            0
   7   train1  GE            26      3       3            0
   8   train2  GE            27      3       4            0
   9   train3  GE            28      3       3            0
```

Figure 7.11 *Continued.*

Another sensitivity what-if analysis might examine the effects of decreasing the overall budget cap from $40K to $30K. This might be due to a need to cut costs because of an unexpected business downturn or perhaps to see if some money can be freed up for an emergency project that has just been sprung. Again, one can make the change to the one constraint in the integer programming code and resolve the problem. Subsequent changes in the portfolio nature and characteristics can then be used to justify any final decision. Figure 7.12 shows the code to do this and Figure 7.13 shows the resulting portfolio and its characteristics.

By examining this new project portfolio versus the original one it is possible to discern differences. The total cost and risk are different but the total gain is not. Also, the coverage of the business directives is different but the coverage of training values remains the same. Finally, one can see that project 16 has been removed from the portfolio and replaced by project 6, which was not funded previously. This kind of information can be valuable in determining whether or not to reduce the Six Sigma project budget cap.

```
data intsens2;
input _id_ $ p1-p20 _type_ $ _rhs_;
cards;
gain 2 10 8 25 5 5 7 11 4 50 16 26 1 3 8 5 5 22 38 9 max .
cost .3 .3 .2 5 1 .8 .2 .7 1 4 8 1.2 .2 .3 .8 .8 1.8 10 10 .9 le
35
risk 25 12 5 50 5 10 25 35 25 35 40 70 70 37 25 12 3 18 80 40 le
250
direct1 1 0 0 1 0 0 0 1 1 0 1 1 0 1 1 0 1 0 1 1 ge 3
direct2 0 1 1 0 0 0 1 0 0 0 0 0 0 0 1 0 1 0 0 0 ge 3
direct3 0 0 0 0 1 1 0 0 0 1 0 0 1 0 0 0 0 0 0 0 ge 3
train1  1 1 0 0 0 1 0 1 1 0 0 0 1 0 0 1 1 0 0 1 ge 3
train2  0 0 1 0 1 0 1 0 0 0 1 0 0 1 1 0 0 1 0 0 ge 3
train3  0 0 0 1 0 0 0 0 0 1 0 1 0 0 0 0 0 0 1 0 ge 3
available 1 1 1 1 1 1 1 1 1 1 1 1 1 1 1 1 1 1 1 1 upperbd .
available 0 0 0 0 0 0 0 0 0 0 0 0 0 0 0 0 0 0 0 0 lowerbd .
integer   1 1 1 1 1 1 1 1 1 1 1 1 1 1 1 1 1 1 1 1 integer .
;
title 'integer sensitivity 2 example';
proc lp data=intsens2;
run;
```

Figure 7.12 Code for integer sensitivity 2.

```
                        Variable Summary

         Variable                                       Reduced
    Col  Name      Status  Type       Price   Activity  Cost
      1  p1                BINARY        2      0         2
      2  p2                BINARY       10      1        10
      3  p3                BINARY        8      1         8
      4  p4                BINARY       25      1        25
      5  p5                BINARY        5      1         5
      6  p6                BINARY        5      1         5
      7  p7                BINARY        7      0         7
      8  p8                BINARY       11      0        11
      9  p9                BINARY        4      0         4
     10  p10               BINARY       50      1        50
     11  p11               BINARY       16      0        16
     12  p12               BINARY       26      0        26
     13  p13               BINARY        1      0         1
     14  p14               BINARY        3      0         3
     15  p15               BINARY        8      1         8
     16  p16               BINARY        5      0         5
     17  p17               BINARY        5      1         5
     18  p18               BINARY       22      1        22
     19  p19               BINARY       38      1        38
     20  p20               BINARY        9      0         9
     21  cost      BASIC   SLACK         0      1.1       0
     22  risk      BASIC   SLACK         0      7         0
```

Figure 7.13 Output for integer sensitivity 2.

```
                            Variable Summary
           Variable                                          Reduced
    Col    Name      Status  Type         Price  Activity    Cost
     23    direct1   BASIC   SURPLUS        0       1          0
     24    direct2   DEGEN   SURPLUS        0       0          0
     25    direct3   DEGEN   SURPLUS        0       0          0
     26    train1    DEGEN   SURPLUS        0       0          0
     27    train2    BASIC   SURPLUS        0       1          0
     28    train3    DEGEN   SURPLUS        0       0          0
integer sensitivity 2 example
                            The LP Procedure
                            Constraint Summary
         Constraint             S/S                          Dual
    Row  Name      Type         Col   Rhs   Activity         Activity
     1   gain      OBJECTVE      .     0      176              .
     2   cost      LE           21    35       33.9            0
     3   risk      LE           22   250      243              0
     4   direct1   GE           23     3        4              0
     5   direct2   GE           24     3        3              0
     6   direct3   GE           25     3        3              0
     7   train1    GE           26     3        3              0
     8   train2    GE           27     3        4              0
```

Figure 7.13 *Continued.*

There is no end to the type of sensitivity questions that might be asked in this manner. If the questions can be formulated as changes in some of the numerical values that are part of the integer programming, then this rerunning of the solution should be capable of providing the analysis in a timely manner. Other questions might be more difficult. For example, if it is suddenly decided that projects 2 and 18 are no longer feasible because of patent contentions, then one must alter the programming code to mimic the changes. It is possible to completely delete the two projects from the code. This means deleting values from every line of the program, resulting in code such as shown in Figure 7.14.

But it is possible (and possibly a little easier) to simply code the gains for projects 2 and 18 to be negative. Then they should never be selected if gain is being maximized. In this example either approach is readily handled, but in complicated problems it is usually preferable to effect the deletion by changing the coefficients rather that the number of entries. See Figure 7.15 for the code that would effect the change in this other way.

There are what-if questions that can be very hard to handle. For example, someone may object to the linear nature or to the way in which the

```
data intreduced;
input _id_ $ p1-p20 _type_ $ _rhs_;
cards;
gain    2  8 25  5  5  7 11  4 50 16 26  1  3  8  5  5 38  9 max .
cost   .3 .2  5  1 .8 .2 .7  1  4  8 1.2 .2 .3 .8 .8 1.8 10 .9 le 40
risk   25  5 50  5 10 25 35 25 35 40 70 70 37 25 12  3 80 40 le 250
direct1 1  0  1  0  0  0  1  1  0  1  1  0  1  1  0  1  1  1 ge 3
direct2 0  1  0  0  0  1  0  0  0  0  0  0  0  1  0  0  0  0 ge 3
direct3 0  0  0  1  1  0  0  0  1  0  0  1  0  0  0  0  0  0 ge 3
train1  1  0  0  0  1  0  1  1  0  0  0  1  0  0  1  1  0  1 ge 3
train2  0  1  0  1  0  1  0  0  0  1  0  0  1  1  0  0  0  0 ge 3
train3  0  0  1  0  0  0  0  0  1  0  1  0  0  0  0  0  1  0 ge 3
available 1 1 1 1 1 1 1 1 1 1 1 1 1 1 1 1 1 1 upperbd .
available 0 0 0 0 0 0 0 0 0 0 0 0 0 0 0 0 0 0 lowerbd .
integer   1 1 1 1 1 1 1 1 1 1 1 1 1 1 1 1 1 1 integer .
;
title 'integer reduced example';
proc lp data=intreduced;
run;
```

Figure 7.14 The sensitivity code for the deletion of two projects.

```
data intreduced1;
input _id_ $ p1-p20 _type_ $ _rhs_;
cards;
gain    2 -10  8 25  5  5  7 11  4 50 16 26  1  3  8  5  5 -22 38  9 max .
cost   .3 .8 .2  5  1 .8 .2 .7  1  4  8 1.2 .2 .3 .8 .8 1.8 10 10 .9 le 40
risk   25 12  5 50  5 10 25 35 25 35 40 70 70 37 25 12  3 18 80 40 le 250
direct1 1  0  0  1  0  0  0  1  1  0  1  1  0  1  1  0  1  0  1  1 ge 3
direct2 0  1  1  0  0  0  1  0  0  0  0  0  0  0  1  0  1  0  0  0 ge 3
direct3 0  0  0  0  1  1  0  0  0  1  0  0  1  0  0  0  0  0  0  0 ge 3
train1  1  1  0  0  0  1  0  1  1  0  0  0  1  0  0  1  1  0  0  1 ge 3
train2  0  0  1  0  1  0  1  0  0  0  1  0  0  1  1  0  0  0  0  0 ge 3
train3  0  0  0  1  0  0  0  0  0  1  0  1  0  0  0  0  0  1  0 ge 3
available 1 1 1 1 1 1 1 1 1 1 1 1 1 1 1 1 1 1 1 1 upperbd .
available 0 0 0 0 0 0 0 0 0 0 0 0 0 0 0 0 0 0 0 0 lowerbd .
integer   1 1 1 1 1 1 1 1 1 1 1 1 1 1 1 1 1 1 1 1 integer .
;
title 'integer reduced 2';
proc lp data=intreduced2;
run;
```

Figure 7.15 A different sensitivity code for the deletion of two projects.

gains are computed, arguing instead that some projects interfere with one another and that the gain really should depend on funding of pairs of projects in a nonlinear formulation. Linear programs can be constructed for a variety of unusual circumstances, but usually such nonlinear formulations require a switch to another kind of programming called nonlinear, which is covered in Chapter 10.

RECIPE FOR THE METHOD USED IN THIS CHAPTER

Integer Programming Method

Step 1 Create linear objective function

Step 2 Create linear constraints

Step 3 Create integer constraints

Step 4 Solve the allocation using integer programming software

Step 5 (Optional but recommended) Perform sensitivity analyses

8
Measuring Portfolio Performance

WHAT IS PORTFOLIO PERFORMANCE?

Now that it has been demonstrated that project portfolios generated by programming methods can be much more efficient than those created by the standard ranking methods, it becomes important to formulate good methods to track the performance of the different approaches. If project selection is to be continuously improved as the Six Sigma philosophy would have it, then it becomes important to track the failings of the different methods so that the process may be improved. The MCDM, AHP, and DEA methods can be checked for poor assumptions about the rankings that were done, in addition to the matching of expectations with reality. The programming methods produce guaranteed optimal portfolios, so performance for them reflects mostly the degree of matching of expectations to results. In either case there are many things that can go awry in the process due to either poor project techniques or unforeseen circumstances. It becomes less and less tolerable to accept poor matches between expectations and results as one takes more and more the attitude that Six Sigma projects are valuable financial instruments. This chapter will introduce methods to evaluate project portfolio performance in ways that can directly contribute to this continuous improvement of the project selection process. Figure 8.1 illustrates that measuring Six Sigma project portfolio performance may involve more than is first perceived.

At first it might seem obvious that one should simply compare the projected gain of the project to the actual gain and call this the performance. This could be a direct comparison of the actual monetary differences in

94 Chapter Eight

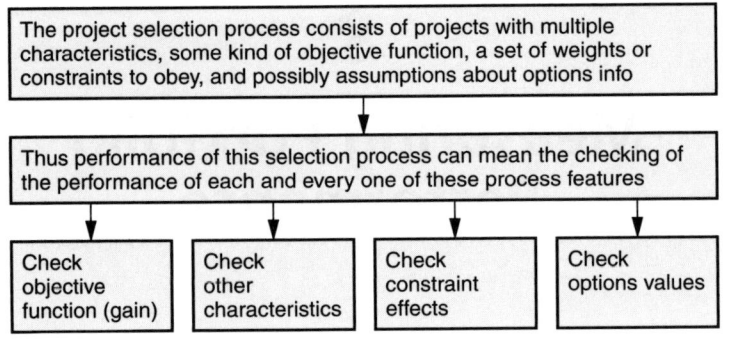

Figure 8.1 The scope of project portfolio performance.

the two amounts or it could be a discrete outcome as to whether the resultant gain was greater than expected or less. This is probably the most common approach that is applied in Six Sigma. There is some inherent value to this approach when it is used with individual projects but it loses some of its impact when used to compare project portfolio performance. This simple comparison will be used as a starting point of a discussion that will lead to better portfolio performance methods.

The comparison of actual to projected gains seems simple but it can be more subtle and complicated than it seems at first. For example, if an individual project fails, then its money may be entirely wasted and no gain produced. But in addition to these losses there is another problem. The money that was wasted on this project, this investment, could have been used to fund a different project that might have succeeded. Should one not account for this opportunity loss as well? Or what if the cost of a particular project exceeds its estimated cost? It is not unusual for projects to overrun their budgets. In fact many companies automatically allow a buffer of say ± five percent that allows for an overrun and still allows a project to be considered on budget. In the case of an overrun like this the company would probably just increase the total money available without necessarily subtracting any funds from other projects. This is equivalent to the original budget cap being greater by some amount. But the project portfolio was chosen to specifically fit within the original constraints. It is possible that an entirely different, and better, portfolio could have been created if the original budget cap had been increased at the time of initial project selection! Perhaps the portfolio should be created with a 'slush fund' project that always gets funded so that money may be taken from it to fund cost overruns in other

- Straight numeric difference between expected and actual gains
- 'Close enough' numeric difference between expected and actual gains
- Count of projects that achieve the target
- Use of risk-adjusted expected gains in the comparison
- Use of a distribution of values
- Recomputing portfolio based on actual gains
- Recomputing portfolio based on several achieved characteristics

Figure 8.2 Some project portfolio performance evaluation methods.

projects. But even this approach could lead to an entirely different project portfolio with a different total gain. Perhaps it is becoming clear from a consideration of these questions that in many ways Six Sigma project portfolio performance analysis shares a great deal in common with sensitivity analysis. It is this similarity between performance and sensitivity analysis that will provide the thread that runs through the remainder of this chapter. A series of approaches useful for Six Sigma project portfolio performance evaluation will be developed and presented in the next sections, ranging from fairly simplistic approaches to reasonably sophisticated ones. The goal of each of these methods is to provide a richer, deeper understanding of project performance so that lessons may be drawn for the improvement of project selection procedure. See Figure 8.2, which shows some of the approaches to project portfolio performance evaluation presented here.

A SIMPLE APPROACH

The naïve approach of simply comparing realized gains to expected gains from a project portfolio certainly makes intuitive sense and is relatively simple, but even in this case there are issues and questions. Consider the 20-project portfolio generated by the integer programming in Chapter 7. The final solution for the fully constrained problem is to fund projects 2 through 6, project 10, project 15, and projects 17 through 19. The expected gain from this portfolio is $176K with a cost of $33.9K and total risk of 245. The business directives are adequately covered with four in directive 1, three in directive 2, and three in directive 3. Likewise, the training objectives are covered with three for Green Belts, four for Black Belts, and three for Master Black Belts. But all these numbers and performances are based on expectations provided by the project leaders before the projects have even begun. It seems wise and even necessary to measure how well the actual project performance matches these expectations.

Assume that the results of the projects are measured according to the company rules for project evaluation. Almost always these rules will include the definition of what kinds of gains and costs should be captured and what time horizon should be used in the evaluation. Clearly it is improbable that any project would meet all its expected gains, expected costs, training values, and business directives exactly. Assume that a measurement of the actual circumstance gives the results shown in Table 8.1, which also shows the expected values for these same quantities.

One possible simple comparison of benefits to results shows that roughly 40 percent of the projects underachieved, 20 percent hit on target, and 40 percent overachieved. This is probably not an unrealistic result for many Six Sigma projects since it is common for unforeseen events to pop up during this kind of aggressive process improvement work. Based on the total gains alone there are $152.2K achieved versus the expected $176K, for a $13.5K underachievement of results. This is the most basic and simplest measure of performance. But it is not the only reasonable way.

Another way to approach the measurement of performance is to check the number of projects that hit their target or at least come within some

Table 8.1 Actual and expected performance of the portfolio.

Project	Expected/ actual gain	Expected/ actual cost	Expected/ actual risk	Expected/ actual directive	Expected/ actual training
2	10/8.5	0.3/0.4	12/0	Two/two	GB/GB
3	8/8.2	0.2/0.3	5/1	Two/two	BB/BB
4	25/20	5.0/4.5	50/0	One/one	MBB/MBB
5	5/5	1.0/1.0	5/1	Three/three	BB/BB
10	50/30	4.0/5.0	35/0	Three/three	MBB/MBB
15	8/10	0.8/2.0	25/1	One/one	MB/MB
16	5/4.5	0.8/0.5	12/1	Two/two	GB/GB
17	5/5	1.8/1.5	3.0/1	One/one	GB/GB
18	22/25	10/12	18/1	Two/two	BB/BB
19	38/36	10/15	80/1	One/one	GB/GB

reasonable interval of the anticipated gain. Often, project estimates are only considered to be within a margin of error at each step of the project regimen. For example, feasibility studies may only be required to be within ±30 percent of the actual cost while final stage approval often depends on estimates that are intended to be within ±10 percent. Such a 'close enough' judgment may be applied to the gain in Figure 8.2 by counting those projects for which the actual gain is within 10 percent of the expected gain. Considered in this way one might conclude that 70 percent of the projects were successful.

Another way to measure success is to choose a slightly different baseline. Since the portfolio was chosen to maintain a low level of risk and to meet the various business directive and training objectives, it might not be the best one could do it if these constraints were not considered in the selection process. In general, constrained portfolios achieve less gain than unconstrained ones. In particular, the average risk of the 10 projects was chosen to be less than about 20 percent chance of failure per project. If one considers an arbitrary portfolio with this level of risk, the expected value of its performance might be better estimated as the 80 percent chance of success times the expected gain of each project. This would result in a computed baseline of 0.80 * $176K = $140.8K. Comparing the achieved total gain of $152.2K to this modified baseline could support the conclusion that the portfolio actually achieved 108 percent of its expected payoff. Clearly this is a much more favorable viewpoint of the Six Sigma project portfolio performance than that given by the simpler approaches.

A Slight Complication

A slight complication can be introduced into this simple expectation-based method. Perhaps one should generate not an expected gain but a distribution of gains and statistically test whether the results are consistent with this distribution of values. This might be done simply by taking the constructed portfolio and providing an estimate of a distribution for each project gain and perhaps for the risk as well. As a simple example of this gain distribution approach consider that each gain is assigned a normal distribution with a standard deviation of one percent of the projected gain value. For example, project 1 would be assigned a normal distribution with a standard deviation of 0.01 * $10K = $0.1K. Consider Table 8.2, which shows the table of projects with a new column showing the associated standard deviation of each gain distribution. Also in the table is an additional column showing a computed value giving a lower cutoff at −3 * standard deviations. Finally, one might consider the set of these lower limits as a baseline

Table 8.2 The expected and achieved project performance.

Project	Expected/ actual gain	Std dev	−3*std dev	Expected/ actual cost	Expected/ actual risk	Expected/ actual directive	Expected/ actual training
2	10/8.5	1.0	7.0	0.3/0.4	12/0	Two/two	GB/GB
3	8/8.2	0.8	5.6	0.2/0.3	5/1	Two/two	BB/BB
4	25/20	2.5	17.5	5.0/4.5	50/0	One/one	MBB/MBB
5	5/5	0.5	3.5	1.0/1.0	5/1	Three/three	BB/BB
10	50/30	5.0	35.0	4.0/5.0	35/0	Three/three	MBB/MBB
15	8/10	0.8	5.6	0.8/2.0	25/1	One/one	MB/MB
16	5/4.5	0.5	3.5	0.8/0.5	12/1	Two/two	GB/GB
17	5/5	0.5	3.5	1.8/1.5	3.0/1	One/one	GB/GB
18	22/25	2.2	15.4	10/12	18/1	Two/two	BB/BB
19	38/36	3.8	26.6	10/15	80/1	One/one	GB/GB

against which to measure the achievements. The baseline given in this way computes as $123.2K. Using this for comparison with the achieved gains gives a performance of $152.2K/$123.2K = 124% of this new expected baseline performance.

Of course another way in which to allow for this type of uncertainty in the estimates is to use lowball estimates in the original project portfolio selection. However, such a modification of the inputs might also change the actual selection of the particular projects in the portfolio, so it could provide very different results.

MOVING TOWARD SENSITIVITY

Although these simple measures of the performance of a Six Sigma project portfolio selection procedure may be adequate for many applications, they do not reveal much about the inner workings of the project selection process. To move toward a more informative measure of performance it seems necessary to construct an approach that incorporates more of the methodology of sensitivity analysis. As a reminder, sensitivity of a portfolio refers to the amount and types of change that can happen in that portfolio when some of the inputs assumptions are altered. One might be interested in the impact of adding more money to the budget or reducing the risk constraint, for example.

There can be a direct link between the questions of sensitivity and those posed in search of a stronger analysis of performance results. A prudent application of sensitivity analysis can be made to create better and more appropriate portfolio baselines against which to judge performance. For example, the actual gains of the projects are known once the projects have been completed. But what if these gains had been available at the time of the portfolio selection? It is quite possible that the entire portfolio might have been different based on these modified gains. And with an entirely new portfolio there might be a considerably different expected gain.

Consider the data on actual gains supplied in Table 8.2. One can rerun the integer programming search with these new gains instead of the original estimates. The new code is given below as Figure 8.3 and the new output as Figure 8.4.

The new Six Sigma project portfolio generated with these better estimates of the projects' gains leads to a portfolio containing projects 2, 3, 5, 6, 10, 12, and 16 through 19. This is different from the original portfolio of projects. The original total gain was estimated to be $176K while this new portfolio has a computed total gain of $153.2K. This is much closer to the actual achieved gain of $152.2K. This might be considered a more suitable baseline for performance evaluation.

```
data c821examp;
input _id_ $ p1-p20 _type_ $ _rhs_;
cards;
gain    2 8.5 8.2 20 5 5 7 11 4 30 16 26 1 3 10 4.5 5 25 36 9 max .
cost    .3 .3 .2 5 1 .8 .2 .7 1 4 8 1.2 .2 .3 .8 .8 1.8 10 10 .9 le 40
risk    25 12 5 50 5 10 25 35 25 35 40 70 70 37 25 12 3 18 80 40 le 250
direct1 1 0 0 1 0 0 0 1 1 0 1 1 0 1 1 0 1 0 1 1 ge 3
direct2 0 1 1 0 0 0 1 0 0 0 0 0 0 0 1 0 1 0 0 ge 3
direct3 0 0 0 0 1 1 0 0 0 1 0 0 1 0 0 0 0 0 0 0 ge 3
train1  1 1 0 0 0 1 0 1 1 0 0 0 1 0 0 1 1 0 0 1 ge 3
train2  0 0 1 0 1 0 1 0 0 0 1 0 0 1 1 0 0 1 0 0 ge 3
train3  0 0 0 1 0 0 0 0 0 1 0 1 0 0 0 0 0 0 1 0 ge 3
available 1 1 1 1 1 1 1 1 1 1 1 1 1 1 1 1 1 1 1 1 upperbd .
available 0 0 0 0 0 0 0 0 0 0 0 0 0 0 0 0 0 0 0 0 lowerbd .
integer   1 1 1 1 1 1 1 1 1 1 1 1 1 1 1 1 1 1 1 1 integer .
;
title 'c8 ex 1';
proc lp data=c821examp;
run;
```

Figure 8.3 The code to generate a new portfolio based on achieved gains.

```
                    Variable Summary
     Variable                                          Reduced
Col  Name    Status  Type       Price   Activity       Cost
  1  p1              BINARY         2          0         -8
  2  p2              BINARY       8.5          1        3.7
  3  p3              BINARY       8.2          1        6.2
  4  p4      DEGEN   BINARY        20          0          0
  5  p5              BINARY         5          1          3
  6  p6              BINARY         5          1          1
  7  p7              BINARY         7          0         -3
  8  p8              BINARY        11          0         -3
  9  p9              BINARY         4          0         -6
 10  p10             BINARY        30          1         16
 11  p11             BINARY        16          0          0
 12  p12             BINARY        26          1         -2
 13  p13             BINARY         1          0        -27
 14  p14             BINARY         3          0      -11.8
 15  p15             BINARY        10          0          0
 16  p16             BINARY       4.5          1       -0.3
 17  p17             BINARY         5          1        3.8
 18  p18             BINARY        25          1       17.8
 19  p19             BINARY        36          1          4
 20  p20             BINARY         9          0         -7
 21  cost    BASIC   SLACK          0        9.9          0
 22  risk            SLACK          0          0       -0.4
 23  direct1 DEGEN   SURPLUS        0          0          0
 24  direct2 BASIC   SURPLUS        0          1          0
 25  direct3 DEGEN   SURPLUS        0          0          0
 26  train1  BASIC   SURPLUS        0          1          0
 27  train2  DEGEN   SURPLUS        0          0          0
 28  train3  DEGEN   SURPLUS        0          0          0
c8 ex 1
                        The LP Procedure
                        Constraint Summary
     Constraint          S/S                        Dual
Row  Name    Type        Col     Rhs   Activity    Activity
  1  gain    OBJECTVE      .       0      153.2        .
  2  cost    LE           21      40       30.1         0
  3  risk    LE           22     250        250       0.4
  4  direct1 GE           23       3          3         0
  5  direct2 GE           24       3          4         0
  6  direct3 GE           25       3          3         0
  7  train1  GE           26       3          4         0
  8  train2  GE           27       3          3         0
  9  train3  GE           28       3          3         0
```

Figure 8.4 The new portfolio based on achieved gains.

FULL SENSITIVITY-BASED PERFORMANCE ANALYSIS

Although some might argue in favor of the recomputed baseline with only the actual gains interposed into the project portfolio selection method, there could be others who argue that one should also update the costs and perhaps even the risk estimates. It is also possible that the business directives and training needs were also incorrectly assigned but this example will include them in the dynamic mostly for demonstration purposes. Again consulting Table 8.1 or 8.2 one can modify the data for the gains, costs, and risks. All the risks for the funded projects that did not meet the rough goals as given by actual risk will be assigned a risk of 100 percent and those that did meet the extended goals will be assigned a risk of zero percent. Similarly, the costs for the funded projects will be replaced by the actual costs. Figure 8.5 shows the code that can be used to rerun the portfolio selection program and Figure 8.6 shows the output for this new optimal Six Sigma project portfolio.

This new Six Sigma project portfolio has projects 3, 5 through 8, 10, 12, 15, and 17 through 19, and a total gain of $168.2K versus the original portfolio with a gain of $176K based on funding the original portfolio of

```
data c822examp;
input _id_ $ p1-p20 _type_ $ _rhs_;
cards;
gain 2 8.5 8.2 20 5 5 7 11 4 30 16 26 1 3 10 4.5 5 25 36 9 max .
cost .3 .4 .3 4.5 1 .8 .2 .7 1 5 8 1.2 .2 .3 2 .5 1.5 12 15 .9 le 40
risk 25 100 0 100 0 10 25 35 25 100 40 70 70 37 0 0 0 0 0 40 le 250
direct1 1 0 0 1 0 0 0 1 1 0 1 1 0 1 1 0 1 0 1 1 ge 3
direct2 0 1 1 0 0 0 1 0 0 0 0 0 0 0 1 0 1 0 0 ge 3
direct3 0 0 0 0 1 1 0 0 0 1 0 0 1 0 0 0 0 0 0 0 ge 3
train1 1 1 0 0 0 1 0 1 1 0 0 1 0 0 1 1 0 0 1 ge 3
train2 0 0 1 0 1 0 1 0 0 0 1 0 0 1 1 0 0 1 0 0 ge 3
train3 0 0 0 1 0 0 0 0 1 0 1 0 0 0 0 0 0 1 0 ge 3
available 1 1 1 1 1 1 1 1 1 1 1 1 1 1 1 1 1 1 1 1 upperbd .
available 0 0 0 0 0 0 0 0 0 0 0 0 0 0 0 0 0 0 0 0 lowerbd .
integer     1 1 1 1 1 1 1 1 1 1 1 1 1 1 1 1 1 1 1 1 integer .
;
title 'c8 ex 2';
proc lp data=c822examp;
run;
```

Figure 8.5 The code to generate a new portfolio with more achieved characteristics.

Chapter Eight

```
                    Variable Summary
     Variable                                        Reduced
Col  Name    Status  Type       Price   Activity     Cost
  1  p1              BINARY       2        0           2
  2  p2              BINARY       8.5      0           8.5
  3  p3              BINARY       8.2      1           8.2
  4  p4              BINARY      20        0          20
  5  p5              BINARY       5        1           5
  6  p6              BINARY       5        1           5
  7  p7              BINARY       7        1           7
  8  p8              BINARY      11        1          11
  9  p9              BINARY       4        0           4
 10  p10             BINARY      30        1          30
 11  p11             BINARY      16        0          16
 12  p12             BINARY      26        1          26
 13  p13             BINARY       1        0           1
 14  p14             BINARY       3        0           3
 15  p15             BINARY      10        1          10
 16  p16             BINARY       4.5      0           4.5
 17  p17             BINARY       5        1           5
 18  p18             BINARY      25        1          25
 19  p19             BINARY      36        1          36
 20  p20             BINARY       9        0           9
 21  cost    BASIC   SLACK        0        0.3         0
 22  risk    BASIC   SLACK        0       10           0
 23  direct1 BASIC   SURPLUS      0        2           0
 24  direct2 DEGEN   SURPLUS      0        0           0
 25  direct3 DEGEN   SURPLUS      0        0           0
 26  train1  DEGEN   SURPLUS      0        0           0
 27  train2  BASIC   SURPLUS      0        2           0
 28  train3  DEGEN   SURPLUS      0        0           0

c8 ex 2
                        The LP Procedure
                      Constraint Summary
     Constraint          S/S                          Dual
Row  Name     Type       Col    Rhs    Activity    Activity
  1  gain     OBJECTVE     .      0     168.2         .
  2  cost     LE          21     40      39.7         0
  3  risk     LE          22    250     240           0
  4  direct1  GE          23      3       5           0
  5  direct2  GE          24      3       3           0
  6  direct3  GE          25      3       3           0
  7  train1   GE          26      3       3           0
  8  train2   GE          27      3       5           0
  9  train3   GE          28      3       3           0
```

Figure 8.6 A new portfolio based on more achieved characteristics.

projects. Again one can use this new total gain as a better baseline against which to measure the actual performance.

OTHER APPROACHES

Many Six Sigma projects, especially if they require major funding or extensive logistical planning, are forced to pass through a series of review steps. Typically there might be an initial selection, a feasibility check, and a final go-ahead. It is possible to halt any project at these stages or to alter its attributes. In most cases the gains, costs, and risks will almost certainly be subject to modification at each of these steps. It is the rare project that does not have any changes made to it over the course of time. Some of the examples presented dealt with situations in which two decisions were made in sequence. There are clear advantages to be gained if one explicitly considers these steps in the portfolio selection procedure. It is important to consider geographical, organizational, or logistical conditions that can affect project performance as well.

Some of the methods described in the next chapter on multiperiod and multidivisional problems might be useful for these kinds of extensions. In addition, a method called *dynamic programming* is well-suited to take advantage of these sequences of project decisions. The penultimate chapter of the book also describes some options and methods that explicitly consider the sequencing of decisions.

9
Multiperiod and Multidivisional Approaches to Six Sigma Project Portfolio Selection

WHAT ARE MULTIPERIOD AND MULTIDIVISIONAL PROBLEMS?

In many Six Sigma project portfolio selection applications there are a few more scenarios that can have significant value but which have not been considered in any detail thus far into this book. One of these options is an allowance for the fact that projects may be part of an integrated plan that extends beyond one year. For example, one project might begin in year one, a different project may start in year two, and a third project start in year three of an integrated three-year planning cycle. This kind of approach is treated under the heading of a multiperiod model below.

The other scenario that can occur is that the situation calls for a multidivisional allocation of projects. This need can occur when project selection boards come from different divisions of the company where the difference might be due to geography or to business process. Most of the time the Six Sigma project portfolio will have to show balance across the different divisional needs. Or the projects may require personnel from different divisions to construct the proper work teams and these scarce resources must be allocated rationally across the projects. Multidivisional project portfolios satisfy these needs by constructing an allocation scheme across the divisions in a manner not too dissimilar to that employed in the multiperiod methods. Ultimately, it is also possible to have portfolios that reflect both multiperiod and multidivisional approaches simultaneously (Hillier 1974).

A Multiperiod Example

Consider once again the 20 potential projects that have been examined in various previous chapters. But now consider that the projects have to be allocated across a three-year planning horizon. Now the Six Sigma project portfolio selection problem morphs will not only construct the optimal set of projects but also will construct the schedule of how to execute those projects over the three years. Notice that this does not imply any precedence of one project over another. If there was a required order to the execution of the projects, the problem would be more amenable to the options approaches of Chapter 11 than to the methods presented in this chapter. Table 9.1 shows the complete inventory of proposed projects, each of which has five characteristics that will have to meet various constraints.

Table 9.1 The 20-project problem characteristics.

Project name	Gain $100K	Cost $100K	% failure	Directive	Training
Project A	2	0.3	25	1	GB
Project C	10	0.3	12	2	GB
Project D	8	0.2	5	2, 3	BB
Project E	25	5.0	50	1, 2, 3	MBB
Project F	5	1.0	5	3	BB
Project G	5	0.8	10	3	GB
Project H	7	0.2	25	2	BB
Project J	11	0.7	35	1	GB
Project K	4	1.0	25	1	GB
Project L	50	4.0	35	3	MBB
Project M	16	8.0	40	1, 2	BB
Project N	26	1.2	70	1, 3	MBB
Project P	1	0.2	70	3	GB
Project Q	3	0.3	37	1	BB
Project R	8	0.8	25	1	BB
Project S	5	0.8	12	2	GB
Project T	5	1.8	3	1	GB
Project U	22	10.0	18	2, 3	BB
Project V	38	10.0	80	1, 2, 3	MBB
Project W	9	0.9	40	1, 3	BB

Along with the constraints on risk there will be a constraint that at least two projects must be chosen from each business directive each year, and there must be at least one project of each belt type in each year. Also, there is a budgetary constraint that no more than $200K may be spent in any given year. A solution portfolio to this problem is a set of projects that should be funded and the years in which they should be active. That is, a schedule is automatically produced as a by-product of this project funding problem.

The multidivisional project selection problem can be handled with the programming methods that have already been introduced in Chapters 6 and 7 by expanding the set of decision variables on which the integer programming method can act. In place of each of the original 20 projects there will now be three variables that combine the project and the year of its scheduled activity. For example, project 18 would be replaced by project 18—year 1, project 18—year 2, and project 18—year 3. The same would be true for the other projects. The integer program will also have more constraints to specify. Instead of a single budget constraint on the whole expenditure there will be three budget constraint specifications, one for each of the three planning horizon years. The other constraints for business directive and for training needs will also be multiplied because of the three years. The integer constraints on the yes/no funding will still be there but now these constraints are applied to each project/year combination. That is, project 1 may only be funded in one of the three years or not at all. The code shown in Figure 9.1 that is necessary to solve this kind of problem is certainly larger and more detailed than previous examples but is not fundamentally more complicated.

The solution of this integer programming problem is shown in Figure 9.2, and one can see on close inspection of the results that it provides a full partitioning of all projects into the three years.

Because of the expansion of each project into three project-year choices it does become more difficult to clearly see that a proper allocation has been accomplished. To see it more clearly, Table 9.2 abstracts the details of the projects and their funding years to emphasize that proper scheduling has been accomplished as part of the selection of the (still!) optimal portfolio of Six Sigma projects.

This project portfolio accommodates the funding of each of the 20 projects over the three-year planning horizon. It also ensures that each project is funded in only one year and that all the constraints are satisfied. While doing all this, it also guarantees that the solution portfolio will be the best one possible for total gain! In particular, that total gain is $2600K, obtained at a total cost over the three years of $77K + 200K + $198K = $475K.

Chapter Nine

```
data mpintexamp;
input _id_ $ y1p1-y1p20 y2p1-y2p20 y3p1-y3p20 _type_ $ _rhs_;
cards;
gain 2 10 8 25 5 5 7 11 4 50 16 26 1 3 8 5 5 22 38 9 2 10 8 25 5
5 7 11 4 50 16 26 1 3 8 5 5 22 38 9 2 10 8 25 5 5 7 11 4 50 16 26
1 3 8 5 5 22 38 9 max .
cost1 .3 .3 .2 5 1 .8 .2 .7 1 4 8 1.2 .2 .3 .8 .8 1.8 10 10 .9 0
0 0 0 0 0 0 0 0 0 0 0 0 0 0 0 0 0 0 0 0 0 0 0 0 0 0 0 0 0 0 0 0
0 0 0 0 0 0 1e 20
cost2 0 0 0 0 0 0 0 0 0 0 0 0 0 0 0 0 0 0 0 0 .3 .3 .2 5 1 .8 .2
.7 1 4 8 1.2 .2 .3 .8 .8 1.8 10 10 .9 0 0 0 0 0 0 0 0 0 0 0 0 0 0
0 0 0 0 0 0 1e 20
cost3 0 0 0 0 0 0 0 0 0 0 0 0 0 0 0 0 0 0 0 0 0 0 0 0 0 0 0 0 0 0
0 0 0 0 0 0 0 0 0 0 .3 .3 .2 5 1 .8 .2 .7 1 4 8 1.2 .2 .3 .8 .8
1.8 10 10 .9 1e 20
risk1 25 12 5 50 5 10 25 35 25 35 40 70 70 37 25 12 3 18 80 40 25
12 5 50 5 10 25 35 25    35 40 70 70 37 25 12 3 18 80 40 25 12 5
50 5 10 25 35 25 35 40 70 70 37 25 12 3 18 80 40 1e 750
direct11 1 0 0 1 0 0 0 1 1 0 1 1 0 1 1 0 1 0 1 1 0 0 0 0 0 0 0 0
0 0 0 0 0 0 0 0 0 0 0 0 0 0 0 0 0 0 0 0 0 0 0 0 0 0 0 0 0 0 0 0
ge 1
direct12 0 0 0 0 0 0 0 0 0 0 0 0 0 0 0 0 0 0 0 0 1 0 0 1 0 0 0 1
1 0 1 1 0 1 1 0 1 0 1 1 0 0 0 0 0 0 0 0 0 0 0 0 0 0 0 0 0 0 0 0
ge 1
direct13 0 0 0 0 0 0 0 0 0 0 0 0 0 0 0 0 0 0 0 0 0 0 0 0 0 0 0 0
0 0 0 0 0 0 0 0 0 0 0 0 1 0 0 1 0 0 0 1 1 0 1 1 0 1 1 0 1 0 1 1
ge 1
direct21 0 1 1 0 0 0 1 0 0 0 0 0 0 0 0 1 0 1 0 0 0 0 0 0 0 0 0 0
0 0 0 0 0 0 0 0 0 0 0 0 0 0 0 0 0 0 0 0 0 0 0 0 0 0 0 0 0 0 0 0
ge 1
direct22 0 0 0 0 0 0 0 0 0 0 0 0 0 0 0 0 0 0 0 0 0 1 1 0 0 0 1 0
0 0 0 0 0 0 1 0 1 0 0 0 0 0 0 0 0 0 0 0 0 0 0 0 0 0 0 0 0 0 0 0
ge 1
direct23 0 0 0 0 0 0 0 0 0 0 0 0 0 0 0 0 0 0 0 0 0 0 0 0 0 0 0 0
0 0 0 0 0 0 0 0 0 1 1 0 0 0 1 0 0 0 0 0 0 0 0 1 0 1 0 0
ge 1
direct31 0 0 0 0 1 1 0 0 0 1 0 0 1 0 0 0 0 0 0 0 0 0 0 0 0 0 0 0
0 0 0 0 0 0 0 0 0 0 0 0 0 0 0 0 0 0 0 0 0 0 0 0 0 0 0 0 0 0 0 0
ge 1
direct32 0 0 0 0 0 0 0 0 0 0 0 0 0 0 0 0 0 0 0 0 0 0 0 0 0 0 1 1 0 0
0 1 0 0 3 0 0 0 0 0 0 0 0 0 0 0 0 0 0 0 0 0 0 0 0 0 0 0 0 0
ge 1
direct32 0 0 0 0 0 0 0 0 0 0 0 0 0 0 0 0 0 0 0 0 0 0 0 0 0 0 0 0
0 0 0 0 0 0 0 0 0 0 0 0 0 1 1 0 0 0 1 0 0 1 0 0 0 0 0 0
ge 1
train11 1 1 0 0 0 1 0 1 1 0 0 0 1 0 0 1 1 0 0 1 0 0 0 0 0 0 0
0 0 0 0 0 0 0 0 0 0 0 0 0 0 0 0 0 0 0 0 0 0 0 0 0 0 0 0 0 0
ge 1
train12 0 0 0 0 0 0 0 0 0 0 0 0 0 0 0 0 0 0 0 0 0 1 1 0 0 0 1 0 1
1 0 0 0 1 0 0 1 1 0 0 1 0 0 0 0 0 0 0 0 0 0 0 0 0 0 0 0 0 0 0
ge 1
train13 1 1 0 0 0 1 0 1 1 0 0 0 1 0 0 1 1 0 0 1 0 0 0 0 0 0 0
0 0 0 0 0 0 0 0 0 0 0 0 0 0 0 0 0 0 0 0 0 0 0 0 0 0 0 0 0 0
ge 1
```

Figure 9.1 The code for a multiperiod integer programming solution.

```
train21    0 0 1 0 1 0 1 0 0 0 1 0 0 1 1 0 0 1 0 0 0 0 0 0 0 0 0 0
           0 0 0 0 0 0 0 0 0 0 0 0 0 0 0 0 0 0 0 0 0 0 0 0 0 0 0 0
ge 1
train22    0 0 0 0 0 0 0 0 0 0 0 0 0 0 0 0 0 0 0 0 0 0 1 0 1 0 1 0
           0 0 1 0 0 1 1 0 0 1 0 0 0 0 0 0 0 0 0 0 0 0 0 0 0 0 0 0
ge 1
train23    0 0 0 0 0 0 0 0 0 0 0 0 0 0 0 0 0 0 0 0 0 0 0 0 0 0 0 0
           0 0 0 0 0 0 0 0 0 0 0 1 0 1 0 1 0 0 0 1 0 0 1 1 0 0 1 0 0
ge 1
train31    0 0 0 1 0 0 0 0 0 1 0 1 0 0 0 0 0 0 1 0 0 0 0 0 0 0 0 0
           0 0 0 0 0 0 0 0 0 0 0 0 0 0 0 0 0 0 0 0 0 0 0 0 0 0 0 0
ge 1
train32    0 0 0 0 0 0 0 0 0 0 0 0 0 0 0 0 0 0 0 0 0 0 0 1 0 0 0 0
           0 1 0 1 0 0 0 0 0 0 1 0 0 0 0 0 0 0 0 0 0 0 0 0 0 0 0 0
ge 1
train33    0 0 0 0 0 0 0 0 0 0 0 0 0 0 0 0 0 0 0 0 0 0 0 0 0 0 0 0
           0 0 0 0 0 0 0 0 0 0 0 0 0 1 0 0 0 0 0 1 0 1 0 0 0 0 0 1 0
ge 1
p1         1 0 0 0 0 0 0 0 0 0 0 0 0 0 0 0 0 0 0 0 0 1 0 0 0 0 0 0
           0 0 0 0 0 0 0 0 0 0 0 0 1 0 0 0 0 0 0 0 0 0 0 0 0 0 0 0
eq 1
p2         0 1 0 0 0 0 0 0 0 0 0 0 0 0 0 0 0 0 0 0 0 0 1 0 0 0 0 0
           0 0 0 0 0 0 0 0 0 0 0 0 0 1 0 0 0 0 0 0 0 0 0 0 0 0 0 0
eq 1
p3         0 0 1 0 0 0 0 0 0 0 0 0 0 0 0 0 0 0 0 0 0 0 0 1 0 0 0 0
           0 0 0 0 0 0 0 0 0 0 0 0 0 0 1 0 0 0 0 0 0 0 0 0 0 0 0 0
eq 1
p4         0 0 0 1 0 0 0 0 0 0 0 0 0 0 0 0 0 0 0 0 0 0 0 0 1 0 0 0
           0 0 0 0 0 0 0 0 0 0 0 0 0 0 0 1 0 0 0 0 0 0 0 0 0 0 0 0
eq 1
p5         0 0 0 0 1 0 0 0 0 0 0 0 0 0 0 0 0 0 0 0 0 0 0 0 0 1 0 0
           0 0 0 0 0 0 0 0 0 0 0 0 0 0 0 0 1 0 0 0 0 0 0 0 0 0 0 0
eq 1
p6         0 0 0 0 0 1 0 0 0 0 0 0 0 0 0 0 0 0 0 0 0 0 0 0 0 0 1 0 0
           0 0 0 0 0 0 0 0 0 0 0 0 0 0 0 0 0 1 0 0 0 0 0 0 0 0 0 0
eq 1
p7         0 0 0 0 0 0 1 0 0 0 0 0 0 0 0 0 0 0 0 0 0 0 0 0 0 0 0 1 0
           0 0 0 0 0 0 0 0 0 0 0 0 0 0 0 0 0 0 1 0 0 0 0 0 0 0 0 0
eq 1
p8         0 0 0 0 0 0 0 1 0 0 0 0 0 0 0 0 0 0 0 0 0 0 0 0 0 0 0 1
           0 0 0 0 0 0 0 0 0 0 0 0 0 0 0 0 0 0 0 1 0 0 0 0 0 0 0 0
eq 1
p9         0 0 0 0 0 0 0 0 1 0 0 0 0 0 0 0 0 0 0 0 0 0 0 0 0 0 0 0
           1 0 0 0 0 0 0 0 0 0 0 0 0 0 0 0 0 0 0 0 1 0 0 0 0 0 0 0
eq 1
p10        0 0 0 0 0 0 0 0 0 1 0 0 0 0 0 0 0 0 0 0 0 0 0 0 0 0 0 0
           0 1 0 0 0 0 0 0 0 0 0 0 0 0 0 0 0 0 0 0 0 1 0 0 0 0 0 0 0
eq 1
p11        0 0 0 0 0 0 0 0 0 0 1 0 0 0 0 0 0 0 0 0 0 0 0 0 0 0 0 0
           0 0 1 0 0 0 0 0 0 0 0 0 0 0 0 0 0 0 0 0 0 0 1 0 0 0 0 0
eq 1
p12        0 0 0 0 0 0 0 0 0 0 0 1 0 0 0 0 0 0 0 0 0 0 0 0 0 0 0 0
           0 0 0 1 0 0 0 0 0 0 0 0 0 0 0 0 0 0 0 0 0 0 0 1 0 0 0 0
eq 1
```

Figure 9.1 *Continued.*

```
p13        0 0 0 0 0 0 0 0 0 0 0 0 1 0 0 0 0 0 0 0 0 0 0 0 0
0 0 0 0 1 0 0 0 0 0 0 0 0 0 0 0 0 0 0 0 0 1 0 0 0 0 0 0 0
eq 1
p14        0 0 0 0 0 0 0 0 0 0 0 0 0 1 0 0 0 0 0 0 0 0 0 0 0
0 0 0 0 0 1 0 0 0 0 0 0 0 0 0 0 0 0 0 0 0 0 1 0 0 0 0 0 0
eq 1
p15        0 0 0 0 0 0 0 0 0 0 0 0 0 0 1 0 0 0 0 0 0 0 0 0 0
0 0 0 0 0 0 1 0 0 0 0 0 0 0 0 0 0 0 0 0 0 0 0 1 0 0 0 0 0
eq 1
p16        0 0 0 0 0 0 0 0 0 0 0 0 0 0 0 1 0 0 0 0 0 0 0 0 0
0 0 0 0 0 0 0 1 0 0 0 0 0 0 0 0 0 0 0 0 0 0 0 0 1 0 0 0 0
eq 1
p17        0 0 0 0 0 0 0 0 0 0 0 0 0 0 0 0 1 0 0 0 0 0 0 0 0
0 0 0 0 0 0 0 0 1 0 0 0 0 0 0 0 0 0 0 0 0 0 0 0 0 1 0 0 0
eq 1
p18        0 0 0 0 0 0 0 0 0 0 0 0 0 0 0 0 0 1 0 0 0 0 0 0 0
0 0 0 0 0 0 0 0 0 1 0 0 0 0 0 0 0 0 0 0 0 0 0 0 0 0 1 0 0
eq 1
p19        0 0 0 0 0 0 0 0 0 0 0 0 0 0 0 0 0 0 1 0 0 0 0 0 0
0 0 0 0 0 0 0 0 0 0 1 0 0 0 0 0 0 0 0 0 0 0 0 0 0 0 0 1 0
eq 1
p20        0 0 0 0 0 0 0 0 0 0 0 0 0 0 0 0 0 0 0 1 0 0 0 0 0
0 0 0 0 0 0 0 0 0 0 0 1 0 0 0 0 0 0 0 0 0 0 0 0 0 0 0 0 1
eq 1
available 1 1 1 1 1 1 1 1 1 1 1 1 1 1 1 1 1 1 1 1 1 1 1 1 1
1 1 1 1 1 1 1 1 1 1 1 1 1 1 1 1 1 1 1 1 1 1 1 1 1 1 1 1 1
upperbd .
available 0 0 0 0 0 0 0 0 0 0 0 0 0 0 0 0 0 0 0 0 0 0 0 0 0
0 0 0 0 0 0 0 0 0 0 0 0 0 0 0 0 0 0 0 0 0 0 0 0 0 0 0 0 0
lowerbd .
integer 1 1 1 1 1 1 1 1 1 1 1 1 1 1 1 1 1 1 1 1 1 1 1 1 1
1 1 1 1 1 1 1 1 1 1 1 1 1 1 1 1 1 1 1 1 1 1 1 1 1 1 1 1 1
integer .
;
title 'integer example';
proc lp data=mpintexamp;
run;
```

Figure 9.1 *Continued.*

```
                    Variable Summary
      Variable                                    Reduced
Col   Name     Status  Type      Price  Activity  Cost
  1   y1p1     DEGEN   BINARY       2      0        0
  2   y1p2     ALTER   BINARY      10      1        0
  3   y1p3     DEGEN   BINARY       8      0        0
  4   y1p4     DEGEN   BINARY      25      0        0
  5   y1p5     BASIC   BINARY       5      1        0
  6   y1p6     DEGEN   BINARY       5      0        0
  7   y1p7     DEGEN   BINARY       7      0        0
  8   y1p8     BASIC   BINARY      11      1        0
  9   y1p9     BASIC   BINARY       4      1        0
 10   y1p10    DEGEN   BINARY      50      0        0
 11   y1p11    DEGEN   BINARY      16      0        0
 12   y1p12    ALTER   BINARY      26      1        0
 13   y1p13    DEGEN   BINARY       1      0        0
 14   y1p14    DEGEN   BINARY       3      0        0
 15   y1p15    ALTER   BINARY       8      1        0
 16   y1p16    DEGEN   BINARY       5      0        0
 17   y1p17    ALTER   BINARY       5      1        0
 18   y1p18    DEGEN   BINARY      22      0        0
 19   y1p19    DEGEN   BINARY      38      0        0
 20   y1p20    ALTER   BINARY       9      1        0
 21   y2p1     ALTER   BINARY       2      0        0
 22   y2p2     DEGEN   BINARY      10      0        0
 23   y2p3     ALTER   BINARY       8      0        0
 24   y2p4     ALTER   BINARY      25      1        0
 25   y2p5     ALTER   BINARY       5      0        0
 26   y2p6     ALTER   BINARY       5      1        0
 27   y2p7     ALTER   BINARY       7      1        0
 28   y2p8     ALTER   BINARY      11      0        0
 29   y2p9     ALTER   BINARY       4      0        0
 30   y2p10    ALTER   BINARY      50      1        0
 31   y2p11    DEGEN   BINARY      16      0        0
 32   y2p12    DEGEN   BINARY      26      0        0
 33   y2p13    DEGEN   BINARY       1      0        0
 34   y2p14    ALTER   BINARY       3      0        0
 35   y2p15    DEGEN   BINARY       8      0        0
 36   y2p16    ALTER   BINARY       5      0        0
 37   y2p17    DEGEN   BINARY       5      0        0
 38   y2p18    ALTER   BINARY      22      1        0
 39   y2p19    ALTER   BINARY      38      0        0
 40   y2p20    DEGEN   BINARY       9      0        0
 41   y3p1     ALTER   BINARY       2      1        0
 42   y3p2     ALTER   BINARY      10      0        0
 43   y3p3     ALTER   BINARY       8      1        0
 44   y3p4     DEGEN   BINARY      25      0        0
 45   y3p5     DEGEN   BINARY       5      0        0
 46   y3p6     ALTER   BINARY       5      0        0
 47   y3p7     ALTER   BINARY       7      0        0
```

Figure 9.2 The output for the multiperiod integer programming problem.

```
integer example
                       The LP Procedure
                       Variable Summary
       Variable                                          Reduced
   Col Name    Status Type      Price   Activity         Cost
    48 y3p8    ALTER  BINARY       11          0             0
    49 y3p9    ALTER  BINARY        4          0             0
    50 y3p10   ALTER  BINARY       50          0             0
    51 y3p11   ALTER  BINARY       16          1             0
    52 y3p12   ALTER  BINARY       26          0             0
    53 y3p13   ALTER  BINARY        1          1             0
    54 y3p14   ALTER  BINARY        3          1             0
    55 y3p15   ALTER  BINARY        8          0             0
    56 y3p16   ALTER  BINARY        5          1             0
    57 y3p17   ALTER  BINARY        5          0             0
    58 y3p18   DEGEN  BINARY       22          0             0
    59 y3p19   ALTER  BINARY       38          1             0
    60 y3p20   ALTER  BINARY        9          0             0
    61 cost1   BASIC  SLACK         0       12.3             0
    62 cost2   ALTER  SLACK         0          0             0
    63 cost3   BASIC  SLACK         0        0.2             0
    64 risk1   BASIC  SLACK         0        128             0
    65 direct11 BASIC SURPLUS       0          5             0
    66 direct12 DEGEN SURPLUS       0          0             0
    67 direct13 BASIC SURPLUS       0          3             0
    68 direct21 ALTER SURPLUS       0          0             0
    69 direct22 BASIC SURPLUS       0          1             0
    70 direct23 BASIC SURPLUS       0          1             0
    71 direct31 ALTER SURPLUS       0          0             0
    72 direct32 BASIC SURPLUS       0          1             0
    73 direct32 ALTER SURPLUS       0          0             0
    74 train11 BASIC  SURPLUS       0          4             0
    75 train12 DEGEN  SURPLUS       0          0             0
    76 train13 BASIC  SURPLUS       0          4             0
    77 train21 BASIC  SURPLUS       0          1             0
    78 train22 BASIC  SURPLUS       0          1             0
    79 train23 BASIC  SURPLUS       0          2             0
    80 train31 ALTER  SURPLUS       0          0             0
    81 train32 BASIC  SURPLUS       0          1             0
    82 train33 DEGEN  SURPLUS       0          0             0
```

Figure 9.2 *Continued.*

```
integer example
                            The LP Procedure
                            Constraint Summary
        Constraint              S/S                              Dual
Row     Name        Type        Col         Rhs     Activity     Activity
  1     gain        OBJECTVE     .            0        260         .
  2     cost1       LE          61           20          7.7       0
  3     cost2       LE          62           20         20         0
  4     cost3       LE          63           20         19.8       0
  5     risk1       LE          64          750        622         0
  6     direct11    GE          65            1          6         0
  7     direct12    GE          66            1          1         0
  8     direct13    GE          67            1          4         0
  9     direct21    GE          68            1          1         0
 10     direct22    GE          69            1          2         0
 11     direct23    GE          70            1          2         0
 12     direct31    GE          71            1          1         0
 13     direct32    GE          72            1          2         0
 14     direct32    GE          73            1          1         0
 15     train11     GE          74            1          5         0
 16     train12     GE          75            1          1         0
 17     train13     GE          76            1          5         0
 18     train21     GE          77            1          2         0
 19     train22     GE          78            1          2         0
 20     train23     GE          79            1          3         0
 21     train31     GE          80            1          1         0
 22     train32     GE          81            1          2         0
 23     train33     GE          82            1          1         0
 24     p1          EQ           .            1          1         2
 25     p2          EQ           .            1          1        10
 26     p3          EQ           .            1          1         8
 27     p4          EQ           .            1          1        25
 28     p5          EQ           .            1          1         5
 29     p6          EQ           .            1          1         5
 30     p7          EQ           .            1          1         7
 31     p8          EQ           .            1          1        11
 32     p9          EQ           .            1          1         4
 33     p10         EQ           .            1          1        50
 34     p11         EQ           .            1          1        16
 35     p12         EQ           .            1          1        26
 36     p13         EQ           .            1          1         1
 37     p14         EQ           .            1          1         3
 38     p15         EQ           .            1          1         8
 39     p16         EQ           .            1          1         5
 40     p17         EQ           .            1          1         5
 41     p18         EQ           .            1          1        22
 42     p19         EQ           .            1          1        38
 43     p20         EQ           .            1          1         9
```

Figure 9.2 *Continued.*

Table 9.2 A schedule of projects through the three years.

Project	Year one	Year two	Year three
1	No	No	Yes
2	Yes	No	No
3	No	No	Yes
4	No	Yes	No
5	Yes	No	No
6	No	Yes	No
7	No	Yes	No
8	Yes	No	No
9	Yes	No	No
10	No	Yes	No
11	No	No	Yes
12	Yes	No	No
13	No	No	Yes
14	No	No	Yes
15	Yes	No	No
16	No	No	Yes
17	Yes	No	No
18	No	Yes	No
19	No	No	Yes
20	Yes	No	No

A MULTIDIVISIONAL EXAMPLE

In a similar way to the multiperiod model, the Six Sigma project portfolio selection may be structured so that it meets interdivisional goals. For example, there may only be a limited number of project managers or Champions to cover all the projects, and the skill sets of these individuals may be distinct enough so that they can not be exchanged. This often happens if the projects are in different areas of the business such as commercial, sales, research, or manufacturing. Consider an example in which the usual 20 projects are required to run in such a way that they can all have the appropriate resources in a single period. There are three resources coming from three different divisions of the company and each resource can only handle three projects each. Otherwise all the original constraints are in effect. Figure 9.3 shows the code and Figure 9.4 the output produced by the integer

```
data mdintexamp;
input _id_ $ d1p1-d1p20 d2p1-d2p20 _type_ $ _rhs_;
cards;
gain 2 10 8 25 5 5 7 11 4 50 16 26 1 3 8 5 5 22 38 9 2 10 8 25 5
5 7 11 4 50 16 26 1 3 8 5 5 22 38 9 max .
cost1 .3 .3 .2 5 1 .8 .2 .7 1 4 8 1.2 .2 .3 .8 .8 1.8 10 10 .9 0
0 0 0 0 0 0 0 0 0 0 0 0 0 0 0 0 0 0 0 0 le 30
cost2 0 0 0 0 0 0 0 0 0 0 0 0 0 0 0 0 0 0 0 0 .3 .3 .2 5 1 .8 .2
.7 1 4 8 1.2 .2 .3 .8 .8 1.8 10 10 .9 le 30
risk1 25 12 5 50 5 10 25 35 25 35 40 70 70 37 25 12 3 18 80 40 25
12 5 50 5 10 25 35 25    35 40 70 70 37 25 12 3 18 80 40 le 750
direct11 1 0 0 1 0 0 0 1 1 0 1 1 0 1 1 0 1 0 1 1 0 0 0 0 0 0 0 0
0 0 0 0 0 0 0 0 0 0 0 0 ge 1
direct12 0 0 0 0 0 0 0 0 0 0 0 0 0 0 0 0 0 0 0 0 0 1 0 0 1 0 0 0 1
1 0 1 1 0 1 1 0 1 0 1 1 ge 1
direct21 0 1 1 0 0 0 1 0 0 0 0 0 0 0 0 1 0 1 0 0 0 0 0 0 0 0 0 0
0 0 0 0 0 0 0 0 0 0 0 0 ge 1
direct22 0 0 0 0 0 0 0 0 0 0 0 0 0 0 0 0 0 0 0 0 0 0 1 1 0 0 0 1 0
0 0 0 0 0 0 1 0 1 0 0 ge 1
direct31 0 0 0 0 1 1 0 0 0 1 0 0 1 0 0 0 0 0 0 0 0 0 0 0 0 0 0 0
0 0 0 0 0 0 0 0 0 0 0 0 ge 1
direct32 0 0 0 0 0 0 0 0 0 0 0 0 0 0 0 0 0 0 0 0 0 0 0 0 1 1 0 0
0 1 0 0 1 0 0 0 0 0 0 0 ge 1
train11 1 1 0 0 0 1 0 1 1 0 0 0 1 0 0 1 1 0 0 1 0 0 0 0 0 0 0 0
0 0 0 0 0 0 0 0 0 0 0 0 ge 1
train12 0 0 0 0 0 0 0 0 0 0 0 0 0 0 0 0 0 0 0 0 1 1 0 0 0 1 0 1
1 0 0 0 1 0 0 1 1 0 0 1 ge 1
train21 0 0 1 0 1 0 1 0 0 0 1 0 0 1 1 0 0 1 0 0 0 0 0 0 0 0 0 0
0 0 0 0 0 0 0 0 0 0 0 0 ge 1
train22 0 0 0 0 0 0 0 0 0 0 0 0 0 0 0 0 0 0 0 0 0 1 0 1 0 1 0
0 1 0 0 1 1 0 0 1 0 0 ge 1
train31 0 0 0 1 0 0 0 0 0 1 0 1 0 0 0 0 0 0 1 0 0 0 0 0 0 0 0 0
0 0 0 0 0 0 0 0 0 0 0 0 ge 1
train32 0 0 0 0 0 0 0 0 0 0 0 0 0 0 0 0 0 0 0 0 0 0 1 0 0 0 0
0 1 0 1 0 0 0 0 0 0 1 0 ge 1
p1       1 0 0 0 0 0 0 0 0 0 0 0 0 0 0 0 0 0 0 0 1 0 0 0 0 0 0 0
0 0 0 0 0 0 0 0 0 0 0 0 eq 1
p2       0 1 0 0 0 0 0 0 0 0 0 0 0 0 0 0 0 0 0 0 0 1 0 0 0 0 0 0
0 0 0 0 0 0 0 0 0 0 0 0 eq 1
p3       0 0 1 0 0 0 0 0 0 0 0 0 0 0 0 0 0 0 0 0 0 0 1 0 0 0 0 0
0 0 0 0 0 0 0 0 0 0 0 0 eq 1
p4       0 0 0 1 0 0 0 0 0 0 0 0 0 0 0 0 0 0 0 0 0 0 0 1 0 0 0 0
0 0 0 0 0 0 0 0 0 0 0 0 eq 1
p5       0 0 0 0 1 0 0 0 0 0 0 0 0 0 0 0 0 0 0 0 0 0 0 0 1 0 0 0
0 0 0 0 0 0 0 0 0 0 0 0 eq 1
p6       0 0 0 0 0 1 0 0 0 0 0 0 0 0 0 0 0 0 0 0 0 0 0 0 0 1 0 0
0 0 0 0 0 0 0 0 0 0 0 0 eq 1
p7       0 0 0 0 0 0 1 0 0 0 0 0 0 0 0 0 0 0 0 0 0 0 0 0 0 0 1 0
0 0 0 0 0 0 0 0 0 0 0 0 eq 1
p8       0 0 0 0 0 0 0 1 0 0 0 0 0 0 0 0 0 0 0 0 0 0 0 0 0 0 0 1
0 0 0 0 0 0 0 0 0 0 0 0 eq 1
p9       0 0 0 0 0 0 0 0 1 0 0 0 0 0 0 0 0 0 0 0 0 0 0 0 0 0 0 0
1 0 0 0 0 0 0 0 0 0 0 0 eq 1
p10      0 0 0 0 0 0 0 0 0 1 0 0 0 0 0 0 0 0 0 0 0 0 0 0 0 0 0 0
0 1 0 0 0 0 0 0 0 0 0 0 eq 1
```

Figure 9.3 The code for the multidivisional integer programming problem.

```
p11       0 0 0 0 0 0 0 0 0 0 1 0 0 0 0 0 0 0 0 0 0 0 0 0 0 0
0 0 1 0 0 0 0 0 0 0 0 0 eq 1
p12       0 0 0 0 0 0 0 0 0 0 0 1 0 0 0 0 0 0 0 0 0 0 0 0 0 0
0 0 0 1 0 0 0 0 0 0 0 0 eq 1
p13       0 0 0 0 0 0 0 0 0 0 0 0 1 0 0 0 0 0 0 0 0 0 0 0 0 0
0 0 0 0 1 0 0 0 0 0 0 0 eq 1
p14       0 0 0 0 0 0 0 0 0 0 0 0 0 1 0 0 0 0 0 0 0 0 0 0 0 0
0 0 0 0 0 1 0 0 0 0 0 0 eq 1
p15       0 0 0 0 0 0 0 0 0 0 0 0 0 0 1 0 0 0 0 0 0 0 0 0 0 0
0 0 0 0 0 0 1 0 0 0 0 0 eq 1
p16       0 0 0 0 0 0 0 0 0 0 0 0 0 0 0 1 0 0 0 0 0 0 0 0 0 0
0 0 0 0 0 0 0 1 0 0 0 0 eq 1
p17       0 0 0 0 0 0 0 0 0 0 0 0 0 0 0 0 1 0 0 0 0 0 0 0 0 0
0 0 0 0 0 0 0 0 1 0 0 0 eq 1
p18       0 0 0 0 0 0 0 0 0 0 0 0 0 0 0 0 0 1 0 0 0 0 0 0 0 0
0 0 0 0 0 0 0 0 0 1 0 0 eq 1
p19       0 0 0 0 0 0 0 0 0 0 0 0 0 0 0 0 0 0 1 0 0 0 0 0 0 0
0 0 0 0 0 0 0 0 0 0 1 0 eq 1
p20       0 0 0 0 0 0 0 0 0 0 0 0 0 0 0 0 0 0 0 1 0 0 0 0 0 0
0 0 0 0 0 0 0 0 0 0 0 1 eq 1
available 1 1 1 1 1 1 1 1 1 1 1 1 1 1 1 1 1 1 1 1 1 1 1 1 1 1
1 1 1 1 1 1 1 1 1 1 1 1 upperbd .
available 0 0 0 0 0 0 0 0 0 0 0 0 0 0 0 0 0 0 0 0 0 0 0 0 0 0
0 0 0 0 0 0 0 0 0 0 0 0 lowerbd .
integer 1 1 1 1 1 1 1 1 1 1 1 1 1 1 1 1 1 1 1 1 1 1 1 1 1 1
1 1 1 1 1 1 1 1 1 1 1 1 integer .
;
title 'integer example';
proc lp data=mdintexamp;
run;
```

Figure 9.3 *Continued.*

programming run for this multidivisional problem. Finally, Table 9.3 summarizes the results. The trick to computing the solution to this multidivisional problem is the same as it was for the multiperiod problem: namely to expand each project into several new project/division inputs. Once this is done, the constraints can be expanded to make sure that the proper allocation of the project/division variables is made.

Table 9.3 summarizes the results of this optimal portfolio that respects the constraints of the different resources across the divisions. Again notice that an appropriate separation is accomplished. The gain from this portfolio is $2600K at a cost of $219K + $256K = $475K. This is the optimal project portfolio for the required conditions. Table 9.3 is provided as an additional aid to emphasize that a valid allocation of the projects has been accomplished by the procedure across the multiple divisions.

```
                         Variable Summary
        Variable                                           Reduced
Col     Name      Status   Type       Price   Activity    Cost
  1   d1p1        ALTER    BINARY        2        0          0
  2   d1p2        ALTER    BINARY       10        0          0
  3   d1p3        ALTER    BINARY        8        0          0
  4   d1p4        ALTER    BINARY       25        0          0
  5   d1p5        ALTER    BINARY        5        0          0
  6   d1p6        ALTER    BINARY        5        0          0
  7   d1p7        ALTER    BINARY        7        0          0
  8   d1p8        ALTER    BINARY       11        0          0
  9   d1p9        ALTER    BINARY        4        0          0
 10   d1p10       ALTER    BINARY       50        0          0
 11   d1p11       ALTER    BINARY       16        0          0
 12   d1p12       ALTER    BINARY       26        0          0
 13   d1p13       BASIC    BINARY        1        1          0
 14   d1p14       ALTER    BINARY        3        0          0
 15   d1p15       ALTER    BINARY        8        0          0
 16   d1p16       BASIC    BINARY        5        1          0
 17   d1p17       ALTER    BINARY        5        0          0
 18   d1p18       BASIC    BINARY       22        1          0
 19   d1p19       BASIC    BINARY       38        1          0
 20   d1p20       BASIC    BINARY        9        1          0
 21   d2p1        BASIC    BINARY        2        1          0
 22   d2p2        BASIC    BINARY       10        1          0
 23   d2p3        BASIC    BINARY        8        1          0
 24   d2p4        BASIC    BINARY       25        1          0
 25   d2p5        BASIC    BINARY        5        1          0
 26   d2p6        BASIC    BINARY        5        1          0
 27   d2p7        BASIC    BINARY        7        1          0
 28   d2p8        BASIC    BINARY       11        1          0
 29   d2p9        BASIC    BINARY        4        1          0
 30   d2p10       BASIC    BINARY       50        1          0
 31   d2p11       BASIC    BINARY       16        1          0
 32   d2p12       BASIC    BINARY       26        1          0
 33   d2p13       ALTER    BINARY        1        0          0
 34   d2p14       BASIC    BINARY        3        1          0
 35   d2p15       BASIC    BINARY        8        1          0
 36   d2p16       ALTER    BINARY        5        0          0
 37   d2p17       BASIC    BINARY        5        1          0
 38   d2p18       ALTER    BINARY       22        0          0
 39   d2p19       ALTER    BINARY       38        0          0
 40   d2p20       ALTER    BINARY        9        0          0
 41   cost1       BASIC    SLACK         0      8.1          0
 42   cost2       BASIC    SLACK         0      4.4          0
 43   risk1       BASIC    SLACK         0      128          0
 44   direct11    BASIC    SURPLUS       0        1          0
 45   direct12    BASIC    SURPLUS       0        8          0
 46   direct21    BASIC    SURPLUS       0        1          0
 47   direct22    BASIC    SURPLUS       0        2          0
```

Figure 9.4 The output for the multidivisional integer programming problem.

```
integer example
                         The LP Procedure
                         Variable Summary
       Variable                                            Reduced
Col Name       Status Type         Price    Activity       Cost
 48 direct31   DEGEN  SURPLUS          0           0          0
 49 direct32   BASIC  SURPLUS          0           2          0
 50 train11    BASIC  SURPLUS          0           2          0
 51 train12    BASIC  SURPLUS          0           5          0
 52 train21    DEGEN  SURPLUS          0           0          0
 53 train22    BASIC  SURPLUS          0           5          0
 54 train31    DEGEN  SURPLUS          0           0          0
 55 train32    BASIC  SURPLUS          0           2          0

integer example
                         The LP Procedure
                         Constraint Summary
     Constraint          S/S                               Dual
Row Name       Type      Col      Rhs   Activity   Activity
  1 gain       OBJECTVE    .        0        260          .
  2 cost1      LE         41       30       21.9          0
  3 cost2      LE         42       30       25.6          0
  4 risk1      LE         43      750        622          0
  5 direct11   GE         44        1          2          0
  6 direct12   GE         45        1          9          0
  7 direct21   GE         46        1          2          0
  8 direct22   GE         47        1          3          0
  9 direct31   GE         48        1          1          0
 10 direct32   GE         49        1          3          0
 11 train11    GE         50        1          3          0
 12 train12    GE         51        1          6          0
 13 train21    GE         52        1          1          0
 14 train22    GE         53        1          6          0
 15 train31    GE         54        1          1          0
 16 train32    GE         55        1          3          0
 17 p1         EQ          .        1          1          2
 18 p2         EQ          .        1          1         10
 19 p3         EQ          .        1          1          8
 20 p4         EQ          .        1          1         25
 21 p5         EQ          .        1          1          5
 22 p6         EQ          .        1          1          5
 23 p7         EQ          .        1          1          7
 24 p8         EQ          .        1          1         11
 25 p9         EQ          .        1          1          4
 26 p10        EQ          .        1          1         50
 27 p11        EQ          .        1          1         16
 28 p12        EQ          .        1          1         26
 29 p13        EQ          .        1          1          1
 30 p14        EQ          .        1          1          3
 31 p15        EQ          .        1          1          8
 32 p16        EQ          .        1          1          5
 33 p17        EQ          .        1          1          5
 34 p18        EQ          .        1          1         22
 35 p19        EQ          .        1          1         38
 36 p20        EQ          .        1          1          9
```

Figure 9.4 *Continued.*

Table 9.3 The summary of the multidivisional integer programming problem.

Project	Resource one	Resource two
1	No	Yes
2	No	Yes
3	No	Yes
4	No	Yes
5	No	Yes
6	No	Yes
7	No	Yes
8	No	Yes
9	No	Yes
10	No	Yes
11	No	Yes
12	No	Yes
13	Yes	No
14	No	Yes
15	No	Yes
16	Yes	No
17	No	Yes
18	Yes	No
19	Yes	No
20	Yes	No

A MULTIDIVISIONAL AND MULTIPERIOD PROBLEM

Of course, real project portfolio selection problems are likely to be both multiperiod and multidivisional in nature. This situation is probably more and more likely to occur in companies who try to create business plans and integrate them as much as feasible with internal and external needs. Just as the multidivisional and the multiperiod approaches were more detailed but not fundamentally different from the standard application of integer programming, so it is true for this still more complicated case. But it, as well, can be readily treated by combining the approaches taken above for each breakdown separately. As an example, consider the 20-project scenario but now with needs to balance the allocation over both time periods and divisional resources. Each of the original 20 variables would have to be expanded into six new variables that combine project, year, and division. Accordingly, new constraints would have to be added to make sure the allocation of these new variables is accomplished in a way that will meet all the requirements. The code and solution are not provided here for this multidivisional/multiperiod situation but, hopefully, it is clear that the code would not look too different from that which has already been presented and simply would have a lot more detail to be specified. Even this expansion of the problem by at least six times should not slow down the solution computation time for most modern integer programming code, but if there were many more projects then some challenges might arise due to the sheer size of the problem.

10
Nonlinear Programming for Six Sigma Project Portfolio Selection

THE NEED FOR NONLINEAR MODELS

Although there is a lot of mileage in the techniques that have been presented to this point, sometimes the linear and integer programming methods are not sufficient for the purpose of selecting Six Sigma project portfolios. This will be the case if the assumption of the linearity in the gain function and in the specification of constraints is substantially incorrect. When either the objective function or the constraints are nonlinear, then the guarantee of optimality that comes with the linear and integer programming methods can fail. In the long, successful history of linear programming applications many powerful methods (Hillier and Lieberman 1974) have been developed that can turn an apparently nonlinear problem into one that can be handled by linear programming, so it is not always necessary to abandon the linear realm. This chapter will introduce a method for handling the optimal selection of project portfolios when the objective or constraints are nonlinear under the assumption that it will be necessary at least for some small set of scenarios.

Nonlinear objective or gain functions could occur quite naturally in the Six Sigma project portfolio selection problem in a number of ways. One situation is when two projects contribute partially to the same gain. For example, perhaps two of the potential projects both impact the same business directive in a similar fashion. This directive might require a two percent improvement in customer satisfaction, raising it from the current 98 percent to the highest possible 100 percent. The directive indicates that such a gain in customer satisfaction is worth $12 million to the company. The first project might be able to raise the percentage to 100 percent by itself whereas the second project can only achieve 99 percent. An objective function that simply adds the two gains from these projects will overcount the possible gain. Clearly the maximum possible gain in this situation is $12 million and yet the sum of the two projects would estimate $12 million + $6 million = $18 million in gain. According to the project attributes list, project 2 will contribute a gain of $1.0 million if it is completed successfully. But project 3 has a projected gain of $0.8 million. In this situation the accumulated gain from two overlapping projects is not a linear combination of the two individual project gains and can be handled with nonlinear programming methods.

Just as there are several approaches or algorithms that can be utilized for linear and integer programming so too are there multiple methods of nonlinear programming. These nonlinear methods are similar to their linear cousins in that they are well-developed, efficient, and have lots of good programming support, but there is one appreciable difference. Nonlinear programs, in general, are not guaranteed to produce the single best solution to the problem. This is because the nonlinear situation is more complicated than the linear situation and the search algorithms can potentially end up in a local minimum rather than the sought-after global minimum. There are many practical ways to avoid this problem such as the strategy of running the nonlinear search algorithm from several different starting points that cover the possibilities of interest, but at heart there is the loss of the theoretical guarantee that was so valuable in the case of linear and integer programming methods. On the other hand, the more complicated situation imposed by nonlinearity usually means that the mathematical portfolio will be even that much better than a simple ranking method–based one.

The algorithms that are used for nonlinear programming can often be tuned to take advantage of specific features of the problem such as the fact that the nonlinear gain function is expressed as a quadratic. But in this book this kind of specialization will be avoided and all examples will be based on one specific general-purpose nonlinear programming algorithm embedded in the SAS NLP (Nonlinear Programming) Procedure code (SAS Institute 1997). In practical problems that relate to Six Sigma project portfolio selection, this method should be easily efficient enough, but it should be remembered that there are other methods that can be of value in very complicated or tremendously large situations. There should still be similarities between the SAS code that is displayed here and other nonlinear programming codes, but the differences are likely to be more noticeable than was true for the linear and integer examples. This greater difference is, again, due to the fundamental complexity of nonlinear optimization. Still, it is expected that the reader can adapt the example code that is given here to their own systems if they want to apply Six Sigma project portfolio selection based on nonlinear programming methods.

A SIMPLE EXPOSITORY EXAMPLE

For ease of introduction to the nonlinear programming methodology, it will help once again to work with a simpler problem than the realistic one presented by 20 projects with numerous constraints. Again the simple example of two projects, A and B, will be used. Recall that project A requires $20K but returns $100K and project B requires $10K and returns $80K. This problem has already been solved using linear and integer programming in previous chapters.

To make this problem nonlinear it will suffice to change the objective from maximizing the gain to maximizing some nonlinear function of the gain. Arbitrarily assume for this problem that this function is given as gain A + gain B − .20 * gain A * gain B, which is a way of constructing an effect of overlap or interaction in the project gain structure. This is the only change that will be made and so there is still assumed to be a total budget constraint of $15K. More complicated problems with more exotic constraints will be considered later. A typical nonlinear programming method might start with an initial guess that is a feasible solution to the problem. For example, setting both investments to $5K satisfies the constraints. Assuming that the projects can be performed under partial funding, Project A gives a benefit of $25K for this investment and project B gives $40K for a total of $65K. The nonlinear function computes to be $25K + $40K − 0.02 * $25K * $40K = $45K. The total cost is of course $10K so there is still money to be spent in hopes of additional gains. The nonlinear programming procedure uses various methods of heuristics to choose a modification of this first portfolio in an attempt to improve it. For example, the method might compute the relative gain of each project and decide it is better to seek to increase project B as much as possible.

One might try to increase the funding for project B an additional $5K, which would use up the entire budget. The performance of this portfolio is $25K + $80K − 0.02 * $25K * $80K = $65K, which is an improvement. So another improvement is tried. Project B is still the best relative gainer, assuming there is no restriction on the amount that can be invested in project B (no integer constraints). This can only be done by stealing money from project A, perhaps to the tune of its entire current $5K funding. Under this new allocation scheme the performance would then be $0K + $120K − 0.02 * $0K * $120K = $120K, which is better still than either of the two previous attempts. But now there does not seem to be any clear way to improve the situation, so the algorithm could stop and proclaim this the optimal value. In this simple problem with a quadratic performance function it is easy to show that this solution is the global maximum but the nonlinear program generally will not be able to provide any guarantee of this fact. The addition of integer constraints to this simple problem does not really change the procedure except that some steps will not be feasible. For example, under the previous scenario, once project B has been fully funded it will be impossible to fund it further or even to partially fund project A. So the search will probably end at this point. This is still the globally optimal solution for this problem. Of course the effectiveness and efficiency of the search will depend greatly on the complexity of the performance function and on the nature of the constraints. To imagine the problem, consider the task of descending a mountain where there are lots of little valleys and dips between summit and bottom. It is easy to get stuck in a dip. Integer and other constraints now make this search process more difficult in ways equivalent to making you walk only to your left. Of course even simple problems like this one can be solved with nonlinear programming code. Figure 10.1 shows the code for the continuous solution of this simple problem and Figure 10.2 the associated output. Figures 10.3 and 10.4 show the code and output respectively for the integer-constrained version.

APPLICATION OF NONLINEAR PROGRAMMING TO A REALISTIC PROBLEM

Consider the 20-project problem with the same constraints that have been established and studied in previous chapters. But now assume that it is utility that is to be maximized rather than the pure benefit. The utility of the project is assumed to be determined by a nonlinear function that has been

```
proc nlp tech=quanew initial=1;
max perf;
parms pa pb;
bounds 0 <= pa pb;
nlcon 0 <= cost <= 15;
perf=pa*100+pb*80-0.02*pa*100*pb*80;
cost=20*pa+10*pb;
run;
```

Figure 10.1 Nonlinear programming continuous code.

```
                    PROC NLP: Nonlinear Maximization
                         Optimization Results
                          Parameter Estimates
                 Gradient      Gradient       Active
                 Objective     Lagrange       Bound
N  Parameter     Estimate      Function       Function     Constraint
1  pa            0             -140.000000    0            Lower BC
2  pb            1.500000      80.000000      0

                 Value of Objective Function = 120
                 Value of Lagrange Function = 120
                 Values of Nonlinear Constraints
                                Lagrange
Constraint        Value         Residual       Multiplier
[  1]  cost_G     15.0000       15.0000        .
[  2]  cost_L     15.0000       0              -8.0000  Active  NLIC
```

Figure 10.2 Nonlinear output for the continuous solution.

```
proc nlp tech=quanew initial=1;
max perf;
parms pa pb;
bounds 0 <= pa pb <=1;
nlc 0 <= cost <= 15;
perf=pa*100+pb*80-0.02*pa*100*pb*80;
cost=20*pa+10*pb;
run;
```

Figure 10.3 Nonlinear code for the integer solution.

```
                    PROC NLP: Nonlinear Maximization
                         Optimization Results
                          Parameter Estimates
                 Gradient      Gradient       Active
                 Objective     Lagrange       Bound
N  Parameter     Estimate      Function       Function     Constraint
1  pa            0             -60.000000     0            Lower BC
2  pb            1.000000      80.000000      0            Upper BC

                 Value of Objective Function = 80
                 Value of Lagrange Function = 80
                 Values of Nonlinear Constraints
                                Lagrange
Constraint        Value         Residual       Multiplier
[  1]  cost_G     10.0000       10.0000        .
[  2]  cost_L     10.0000       5.0000         .
```

Figure 10.4 Nonlinear programming output for the integer solution.

Table 10.1 The proposed projects with utility.

Name	Gain $100K	Cost $100K	Failure %	Directive	Training	Utility
Project A	2	0.3	25	1	GB	5.0000
Project C	10	0.3	12	2	GB	29.3333
Project D	8	0.2	5	2, 3	BB	38.0000
Project E	25	5.0	50	1, 2, 3	MBB	2.5000
Project F	5	1.0	5	3	BB	4.7500
Project G	5	0.8	10	3	GB	5.6250
Project H	7	0.2	25	2	BB	26.2500
Project J	11	0.7	35	1	GB	10.2143
Project K	4	1.0	25	1	GB	3.0000
Project L	50	4.0	35	3	MBB	8.1250
Project M	16	8.0	40	1, 2	BB	1.2000
Project N	26	1.2	70	1, 3	MBB	6.5000
Project P	1	0.2	70	3	GB	1.5000
Project Q	3	0.3	37	1	BB	6.3000
Project R	8	0.8	25	1	BB	7.5000
Project S	5	0.8	12	2	GB	5.5000
Project T	5	1.8	3	1	GB	2.6944
Project U	22	10.0	18	2, 3	BB	1.8040
Project V	38	10.0	80	1, 2, 3	MBB	0.7600
Project W	9	0.9	40	1, 3	B	6.0000

developed by the company and is given as (1 − failure/100) * (gain/cost). Table 10.1 repeats the original data associated with the Six Sigma 20-project portfolio selection problem that has been used as an example several times already in this book, with an additional column added showing this utility.

Figure 10.5 shows the code to solve this problem with the integer constraints and Figure 10.6 shows the output of the programming run.

Notice that every project is assigned a weight in this optimal portfolio but it easy to see which ones should have zero weights, that is, not be funded. Specifically, this Six Sigma project portfolio consists of projects 2 through 8, 10, and 12, which achieves a best value of 10.88 at a cost of $135K. The total achieved risk is 247.

Nonlinear Programming for Six Sigma Project Portfolio Selection 127

```
proc nlp tech=quanew initial=1;
parms p1 p2 p3 p4 p5 p6 p7 p8 p9 p10 p11 p12 p13 p14 p15 p16 p17
p18 p19 p20;
bounds 0 <= p1 p2 p3 p4 p5 p6 p7 p8 p9 p10 p11 p12 p13 p14 p15
p16 p17 p18 p19 p20 <=1;
nlincon
ct <= 40,
rk <= 300,
d1 <= 3,
d2 >= 3,
d3 >= 3,
tb >= 3,
tbb >= 3,
tmb >= 3;
lcon p7+p13=1;
max roi;
gn1=p1*2.+p2*10.+p3*8.+p4*25.+p5*5.+p6*5.+p7*7.+p8*11.+p9*4.+p10*
50.+p11*16.;
gn2=p12*26.+p13*1.+p14*3.+p15*8.+p16*5.+p17*5.+p18*22.+p19*38.+p
20*9.;
gn=gn1+gn2;
ct1=p1*.3+p2*.3+p3*.2+p4*5.+p5*1.+p6*.9+p7*.2+p8*.7+p9*1.+p10*4.;
ct2=p11*8.+p12*1.2+p13*.2+p14*.3+p15*.8+p16*.8+p17*1.8+p18*10.+p1
9*10.+p20*.9;
ct=ct1+ct2;
roi=gn/ct;
rk=p1*25+p2*12+p3*5+p4*50+p5*5+p6*10+p7*25+p8*35+p9*25+p10*35+
p11*40+p12*70+p13*70+p14*37+p15*25+p16*12+p17*3+p18*18+p19*80+p2
0*40;
rg=rk*roi;
rv=p1*(25-30)**2+p2*(12-30)**2+p3*(5-30)**2+p4*(50-30)**2+
p5*(5-30)**2+p6*(10-30)**2+p7*(25-30)**2+p8*(35-30)**2+p9*(25-
30)**2+
p10*(35-30)**2+p11*(40-30)**2+p12*(70-30)**2+p13*(70-
30)**2+p14*(37-30)**2+
p15*(25-30)**2+p16*(12-30)**2+p17*(3-30)**2+p18*(18-
30)**2+p19*(80-30)**2+
p20*(40-30)**2;
d1=p1+p4+p8+p9+p11+p12+p14+p15+p17+p19+p20;
d2=p2+p3+p7+p16+p18+p20;
d3=p5+p6+p10+p13;
tb=p1+p2+p6+p8+p9+p13+p16+p17;
tbb=p3+p5+p7+p11+p14+p15+p18+p20;
tmb=p4+p10+p12+p19;
utility=roi;
run;
```

Figure 10.5 The nonlinear programming code with utility.

```
              PROC NLP: Nonlinear Maximization
                     Optimization Results
                     Parameter Estimates
                Gradient         Gradient    Active
                Objective        Lagrange    Bound
  N Parameter   Estimate         Function    Function   Constraint
  1  p1         -2.10734E-11    -0.093827    0          Lower BC
  2  p2          1.000000        0.498765    0          Upper BC
  3  p3          1.000000        0.431276    0          Upper BC
  4  p4          1.000000       -2.181070    0          Upper BC
  5  p5          1.000000       -0.436214    0          Upper BC
  6  p6          1.000000       -0.355556    0          Upper BC
  7  p7          1.000000        0.357202    0          Upper BC
  8  p8          1.000000        0.250206    0          Upper BC
  9  p9         -3.16101E-11     0.510288    0          Lower BC
 10  p10         1.000000        0.477366    0          Upper BC
 11  p11        -3.16101E-11    -5.267490    0          Lower BC
 12  p12         1.000000        0.958025    0          Upper BC
 13  p13         5.268397E-12   -0.087243    0          Lower BC LinDep
 14  p14         8.429371E-11   -0.019753    0          Lower BC
 15  p15         0              -0.052675    0          Lower BC
 16  p16         5.795187E-11   -0.274897    0          Lower BC
 17  p17        -3.16101E-11    -1.081481    0          Lower BC
 18  p18        -3.16101E-11    -6.436214    0          Lower BC
 19  p19        -2.10734E-11    -5.251029    0          Lower BC
 20  p20         0              -0.059259    0          Lower BC

           Value of Objective Function = 10.888888889
           Value of Lagrange Function = 10.888888889

           Linear Constraints Evaluated at Solution
    1 ACT - 5.551E - 17 = -1.0000 + 1.0000 * p7 + 1.0000 * p13

                 Values of Nonlinear Constraints
                                  Lagrange
  Constraint       Value          Residual    Multiplier
  [  2]  ct_L      13.5000        26.5000        .
  [  3]  rk_L      247.0          53.0000        .
  [  4]  d1_L      3.0000         0              . Active  NLIC  LinDep
  [  5]  d2_G      3.0000         6.32E-11       . Active  NLIC  LinDep
  [  6]  d3_G      3.0000        -444E-18        . Active  NLIC  LinDep
  [  7]  tb_G      3.0000         0              . Active  NLIC  LinDep
  [  8]  tbb_G     3.0000        -444E-18        . Active  NLIC  LinDep
  [  9]  tmb_G     3.0000         6.32E-11       . Active  NLIC  LinDep
```

Figure 10.6 The nonlinear output for the utility example.

THE ADDITION OF A NONLINEAR CONSTRAINT

Another way in which the problem can become nonlinear is for one or more constraints to be nonlinear in form. For this example one could still maximize ROI but make the project portfolio selection subject to the additional constraint that risk * cost < 100.

Figure 10.7 shows the code that can be used to solve this problem and Figure 10.8 shows the output.

```
proc nlp tech=quanew initial=1;
parms p1 p2 p3 p4 p5 p6 p7 p8 p9 p10 p11 p12 p13 p14 p15 p16 p17
p18 p19 p20;
bounds 0 <= p1 p2 p3 p4 p5 p6 p7 p8 p9 p10 p11 p12 p13 p14 p15
p16 p17 p18 p19 p20 <=1;
nlincon
ct <= 40,
rk <= 300,
rc <= 1000,
d1 <= 3,
d2 >= 3,
d3 >= 3,
tb >= 3,
tbb >= 3,
tmb >= 3;
lcon p7+p13=1;
max roi;
gn1=p1*2.+p2*10.+p3*8.+p4*25.+p5*5.+p6*5.+p7*7.+p8*11.+p9*4.+p10*
50.+p11*16.;
gn2=p12*26.+p13*1.+p14*3.+p15*8.+p16*5.+p17*5.+p18*22.+p19*38.+p
20*9.;
gn=gn1+gn2;
ct1=p1*.3+p2*.3+p3*.2+p4*5.+p5*1.+p6*.9+p7*.2+p8*.7+p9*1.+p10*4.;
ct2=p11*8.+p12*1.2+p13*.2+p14*.3+p15*.8+p16*.8+p17*1.8+p18*10.+p1
9*10.+p20*.9;
ct=ct1+ct2;
roi=gn/ct;
rk=p1*25+p2*12+p3*5+p4*50+p5*5+p6*10+p7*25+p8*35+p9*25+p10*35+p11
*40+p12*70+p13*70+p14*37+p15*25+p16*12+p17*3+p18*18+p19*80+p20*40;
rg=rk*roi;
rc=(1-(rk/100))*ct;
rv=p1*(25-30)**2+p2*(12-30)**2+p3*(5-30)**2+p4*(50-30)**2+p5*
(5-30)**2+p6*(10-30)**2+p7*(25-30)**2+p8*(35-30)**2+p9*(25-30)**
2+p10*(35-30)**2+p11*(40-30)**2+p12*(70-30)**2+p13*(70-30)**
2+p14*(37-30)**2+p15*(25-30)**2+p16*(12-30)**2+p17*(3-30)**2+p18*
(18-30)**2+p19*(80-30)**2+p20*(40-30)**2;
d1=p1+p4+p8+p9+p11+p12+p14+p15+p17+p19+p20;
d2=p2+p3+p7+p16+p18+p20;
```

Figure 10.7 The code for the nonlinear problem with a nonlinear constraint.

130 Chapter Ten

```
d3=p5+p6+p10+p13;
tb=p1+p2+p6+p8+p9+p13+p16+p17;
tbb=p3+p5+p7+p11+p14+p15+p18+p20;
tmb=p4+p10+p12+p19;
utility=roi;
run;
```

Figure 10.7 *Continued.*

Optimization Results
Parameter Estimates

N	Parameter	Gradient Objective Estimate	Gradient Lagrange Function	Active Bound Function	Constraint	
1	p1	-2.10734E-11	-0.093827	0	Lower BC	
2	p2	1.000000	0.498765	0	Upper BC	
3	p3	1.000000	0.431276	0	Upper BC	
4	p4	1.000000	-2.181070	0	Upper BC	
5	p5	1.000000	-0.436214	0	Upper BC	
6	p6	1.000000	-0.355556	0	Upper BC	
7	p7	1.000000	0.357202	0	Upper BC	
8	p8	1.000000	0.250206	0	Upper BC	
9	p9	-3.16101E-11	-0.510288	0	Lower BC	
10	p10	1.000000	0.477366	0	Upper BC	
11	p11	-3.16101E-11	-5.267490	0	Lower BC	
12	p12	1.000000	0.958025	0	Upper BC	
13	p13	5.268397E-12	-0.087243	0	Lower BC	LinDep
14	p14	8.429371E-11	-0.019753	0	Lower BC	
15	p15	0	-0.052675	0	Lower BC	
16	p16	5.795187E-11	-0.274897	0	Lower BC	
17	p17	-3.16101E-11	-1.081481	0	Lower BC	
18	p18	-3.16101E-11	-6.436214	0	Lower BC	
19	p19	-2.10734E-11	-5.251029	0	Lower BC	
20	p20	0	-0.059259	0	Lower BC	

Value of Objective Function = 10.888888889

Value of Lagrange Function = 10.888888889

Linear Constraints Evaluated at Solution
1 ACT - 5.551E - 17 = -1.0000 + 1.0000 * p7 + 1.0000 * p13

Values of Nonlinear Constraints

Constraint		Value	Lagrange Residual	Multiplier		
[2]	ct_L	13.5000	26.5000	.		
[3]	rk_L	247.0	53.0000	.		
[4]	rc_L	-19.8450	1019.8	.		
[5]	d1_L	3.0000	0	. Active	NLIC	LinDep
[6]	d2_G	3.0000	6.32E-11	. Active	NLIC	LinDep
[7]	d3_G	3.0000	-444E-18	. Active	NLIC	LinDep
[8]	tb_G	3.0000	0	. Active	NLIC	LinDep

Figure 10.8 The output for the nonlinear problem with a nonlinear constraint.

NONLINEAR SENSITIVITY ANALYSIS

In spite of the fact that in this nonlinear situation there is still the same need to examine the sensitivity of the solution portfolio to the assumptions that are made in the model coefficients and structure. This is probably most easily accomplished in nonlinear programming by simply making appropriate changes in the code and then recomputing the solution. As an example, let's examine the code wherein the gain for project 1 is changed from $2.0K to $3.0K. Figure 10.9 shows the SAS procedure NLP code and Figure 10.10 gives the solution details.

```
proc nlp tech=quanew initial=1;
parms p1 p2 p3 p4 p5 p6 p7 p8 p9 p10 p11 p12 p13 p14 p15 p16 p17
p18 p19 p20;
bounds 0 <= p1 p2 p3 p4 p5 p6 p7 p8 p9 p10 p11 p12 p13 p14 p15
p16 p17 p18 p19 p20 <=1;
nlincon
ct <= 40,
rk <= 300,
rc <= 1000,
d1 <= 3,
d2 >= 3,
d3 >= 3,
tb >= 3,
tbb >= 3,
tmb >= 3;
lcon p7+p13=1;
max roi;
gn1=p1*3.+p2*10.+p3*8.+p4*25.+p5*5.+p6*5.+p7*7.+p8*11.+p9*4.+p10*
50.+p11*16.;
gn2=p12*26.+p13*1.+p14*3.+p15*8.+p16*5.+p17*5.+p18*22.+p19*38.+p
20*9.;
gn=gn1+gn2;
ct1=p1*.3+p2*.3+p3*.2+p4*5.+p5*1.+p6*.9+p7*.2+p8*.7+p9*1.+p10*4.;
ct2=p11*8.+p12*1.2+p13*.2+p14*.3+p15*.8+p16*.8+p17*1.8+p18*10.+p1
9*10.+p20*.9;
ct=ct1+ct2;
roi=gn/ct;
rk=p1*25+p2*12+p3*5+p4*50+p5*5+p6*10+p7*25+p8*35+p9*25+p10*35+
p11*40+p12*70+p13*70+p14*37+p15*25+p16*12+p17*3+p18*18+p19*80+p2
0*40;
rg=rk*roi;
rc=(1-(rk/100))*ct;
rv=p1*(25-30)**2+p2*(12-30)**2+p3*(5-30)**2+p4*(50-30)**2+p5*
(5-30)**2+p6*(10-30)**2+p7*(25-30)**2+p8*(35-30)**2+p9*(25-30)**
2+p10*(35-30)**2+p11*(40-30)**2+p12*(70-30)**2+p13*(70-30)**2+p14*
(37-30)**2+p15*(25-30)**2+p16*(12-30)**2+p17*(3-30)**2+p18*
(18-30)**2+p19*(80-30)**2+p20*(40-30)**2;
d1=p1+p4+p8+p9+p11+p12+p14+p15+p17+p19+p20;
d2=p2+p3+p7+p16+p18+p20;
```

Figure 10.9 The code for the nonlinear sensitivity analysis.

132 Chapter Ten

```
d3=p5+p6+p10+p13;
tb=p1+p2+p6+p8+p9+p13+p16+p17;
tbb=p3+p5+p7+p11+p14+p15+p18+p20;
tmb=p4+p10+p12+p19;
utility=roi;
run;
```

Figure 10.9 *Continued.*

```
                        Optimization Results
                        Parameter Estimates

                Gradient        Gradient   Active
                Objective       Lagrange   Bound
  N Parameter   Estimate        Function   Function      Constraint
  1 p1          -1.05367E-11    -0.019753  0             Lower BC
  2 p2           1.000000        0.498765  0             Upper BC
  3 p3           1.000000        0.431276  0             Upper BC
  4 p4           1.000000       -2.181070  0             Upper BC
  5 p5           1.000000       -0.436214  0             Upper BC
  6 p6           1.000000       -0.355556  0             Upper BC
  7 p7           1.000000        0.357202  1.387779E-17  Upper BC
  8 p8           1.000000        0.250206  0             Upper BC
  9 p9          -3.16101E-11    -0.510288  0             Lower BC
 10 p10          1.000000        0.477366  0             Upper BC
 11 p11         -3.16101E-11    -5.267490  0             Lower BC
 12 p12          1.000000        0.958025  0             Upper BC
 13 p13          0              -0.087243  0             Lower BC LinDep
 14 p14          7.375724E-11   -0.019753  0             Lower BC
 15 p15          0              -0.052675  0             Lower BC
 16 p16          5.268358E-11   -0.274897  0             Lower BC
 17 p17         -3.16101E-11    -1.081481  0             Lower BC
 18 p18         -3.16101E-11    -6.436214  0             Lower BC
 19 p19         -2.10734E-11    -5.251029  0             Lower BC
 20 p20          0              -0.059259  0             Lower BC

          Value of Objective Function = 10.888888889

          Value of Lagrange Function = 10.888888889

          Linear Constraints Evaluated at Solution
       1 ACT 0 = -1.0000 + 1.0000 * p7 + 1.0000 * p13

                Values of Nonlinear Constraints

                                  Lagrange
   Constraint       Value         Residual    Multiplier
   [ 2]  ct_L       13.5000       26.5000     .
   [ 3]  rk_L       247.0         53.0000     .
   [ 4]  rc_L       -19.8450      1019.8      .
   [ 5]  d1_L       3.0000        0           . Active   NLIC    LinDep
   [ 6]  d2_G       3.0000        6.32E-11    . Active   NLIC    LinDep
   [ 7]  d3_G       3.0000        0           . Active   NLIC    LinDep
   [ 8]  tb_G       3.0000        0           . Active   NLIC    LinDep
```

Figure 10.10 The output for the nonlinear sensitivity analysis.

In this case there is no change to the structure of the project portfolio caused by the change in cost of the first project, although there are slight numerical changes in the various values. Through application of this change and rerun approach it should be possible to examine just about every sensitivity issue that might arise in the course of Six Sigma project portfolio selection. Of course, depending on the depth of the sensitivity question, more or less dramatic alterations may have to be inserted into the code.

RECIPE FOR THE METHOD USED IN THIS CHAPTER

Nonlinear Programming

Step 1 Create the appropriate nonlinear objective function

Step 2 Construct the possible nonlinear constraints

Step 3 Compute solutions

Step 4 (Optional but recommended) Rerun from different starting points

Step 5 (Optional but recommended) Run sensitivity studies

11
Options Pricing Approaches to Six Sigma Project Portfolio Selection

THE NEED FOR DYNAMIC ALLOCATION

Although the many methods that have been presented so far in this book for the purpose of Six Sigma project portfolio selection are likely to give significant advantages over the standard project-by-project ranked approach, there are some limitations associated with them that should be considered. One of these limitations comes from the fact that the portfolio is selected at a single point in time. In computer programming parlance this might be called batch processing as compared to interactive processing. There is no opportunity or at least no consideration made of the fact that many projects have to pass through a sequence of checkpoints on their way to completion. For example, it is quite common for a Six Sigma project to be reviewed by management as it passes certain phases. At each phase any of the project particulars are open to modification as well as the viability of the entire project itself. These stages often include project conception, feasibility, adoption, and evaluation phases. At each stage there are likely to be different conditions required on the provided estimates of cost, benefit, and risk. The estimates of these characteristics may need to be made more precise at each stage as well. Similarly, the methods of project management may be changed as well as project team members or support resources. The management team may respond to these modifications in each project by increasing or decreasing funding. They may even choose to add or delete entire projects from the portfolio, which would in turn potentially affect the guarantees and returns of this carefully selected set of projects.

This addition of the sequencing of opportunities to make dynamic changes is a key ingredient of many practical Six Sigma projects that is not fully encompassed by the static methods that have been developed thus far. Fortunately there are several good ways to improve these static methods and help make the Six Sigma project portfolio selection process more dynamic. As a general rule, this close agreement between the actual selection process and the methods that guide the process should make it more likely that significant improvements can be made in the portfolios and therefore in the project results. Most of the dynamic methods fall into one of three categories: dynamic programming, decision analysis, and options pricing methods. Only the options pricing approach will be detailed here. But this is not an important restriction since all three methods can be similar in their application and can be mixed and matched to make even more sophisticated approaches.

WHAT OPTIONS ARE

Options originated as financial instruments (Broadie and Detemple 2004) that allow investors to buy a stock or bond at a prefixed price at some definite time in the future or to choose not to buy it at all. Because the decision to buy or not to buy is made in the future there is uncertainty as to what the actual value of the commodity will be at the point of purchase. The option allows the investors, for a price, to buy if the future price has increased favorably or to not buy if a decrease has occurred. The option allows the investor to avoid an investment that will lose him money and therefore to avoid the downside of the investment. For example, a woman has $100,000 available for investment today. She could buy stocks, let them ride and take whatever benefit accrues over the horizon of a year. At the end of the year the stock values may have increased and she will make money. Or at the end of the year the values of the stocks may have decreased and she will have lost money. That is, she will have lost money unless she has the option to not sell the stock at the end of the year. In the case of a market downturn the woman will likely not sell her stocks and this knowledge of how the future actually developed allows her to avoid the downside of her investment.

Financial options are very popular instruments because they allow one to gain control of risk and potentially to eliminate it when this approach is applied in isolation or when it is combined with hedging and diversification. Financial options are available in a bewildering array of flavors including American, European, and Asian options. Some versions allow the exercise of the options at any time during the time interval up to a maximum point. Some allow the investor to exercise the options at only one point in time.

Still others allow the exercise at multiple scheduled times only. Options may be placed on stocks, bonds, real estate, or any other vehicle where there is an element of risk engendered by the passage of time. The pricing of an option is a critical feature that tries to encapsulate all this future risk in one value at one particular point in time.

Perhaps it is already clear that the options approach to thinking about risk can be applied as well to Six Sigma project portfolio selection. Each project has a risk that it will not achieve what is expected. For example, the project may fail completely, or it may achieve only 50 percent of its anticipated gain, or it may unexpectedly achieve double its nominal value. Most managers would gladly pay a premium up front if it would ensure that this kind of risk is mitigated. This implies that if one can properly value each project as an option, this may provide a useful input to the portfolio selection procedure. This attempt to control the impact of risk on a company investment is called a real option (Bowman and Moskowitz 2001). In the contest of Six Sigma project portfolio selection processes real options may be used to set priorities, to suggest modification of project characteristics, or to provide a different input to the linear or integer program. The discussion of real options pricing that is given in this book will be primarily concerned with setting a good price that can be used as input to the portfolio selection process but there are more extensive uses for aggressive project management that can be undertaken as well (Smith and Nau 1995).

A SIMPLE OPTIONS PRICING APPROACH TO PROJECT SELECTION

To better illustrate the options process before application to a realistic portfolio of projects, consider the two-project example that has been examined in previous chapters. There are two projects, A and B, with costs $20K and $10K respectively. The expected gains of these two projects are $100K and $80K, respectively, and the only constraint is a budget cap of $15K. To frame this as an options problem consider first project A.

At the first review meeting, say the feasibility meeting, there are at least two actions that are possible: fund the project now or do not fund the project now. If the project is funded then at the end of one year the project is expected to be completed and the gain can be harvested. That is, the choice to fund the project at feasibility is similar to the action of buying an option that will allow the purchase of the full gain one year later at the original price. The actual value of the project at the end of the year could be different from the anticipated gain for any of a variety of reasons such as poor planning, business conditions, unexpected resource limitations, technical problems, or customer dynamics. It seems to make some sense to give preferential funding to those projects with higher options prices.

This logic can be rewritten as a table of values. Table 11.1 shows how the various costs and values might be assigned for this simple options case.

The options approach tries to take into account the uncertainty inherent in the project values in the unknown future. It does this by first computing the net present value (NPV) of each outcome. Net present value is a common financial computation that attempts to allow for the financial costs of action taken today for future benefits. NPV for this simple example is equal to the final value discounted by a typical interest rate with the cost subtracted out. If one chooses say 10 percent discounting then the NPV for the fund – increase outcome is ($120K/1.10) – $20K = $89.09. Similarly the outcome for fund – decrease has an NPV of ($80K/1.10) – $20K = $52.72. The final branch for not funding the project of course has NPV = $0K. Table 11.2 shows the additional NPV column added to the original description.

To combine these various possibilities into an options-based price, the next step is to compute the probability that the project will increase or decrease. In very general problems one can specify this based on company history and opinion but for now one can take a more neutral approach. If PINC is the probability of an increase in value then the basic computation is PINC * $120K + (1 – PINC) * $80K = 1.10 * $100K with a solution for

Table 11.1 Logic of the simple options example.

Branch	Cost step 1	Value at step 2	Value–cost at step 2
Fund—increase	$20K	$120K	$100K
Fund—decrease	$20K	$80K	$60K
Do not fund	$0K	$0K	$0K

Table 11.2 The simple options example with NPV.

Branch	Cost step 1	Value at step 2	Value–cost at step 2	NPV
Fund—increase	$20K	$120K	$100K	$89.09K
Fund—decrease	$20K	$80K	$60K	$52.72K
Do not fund	$0K	$0K	$0K	$0 K

PINC of $30K/$40K = 0.75. Using this newly computed PINC one can simply compute a weighted average of the NPVs with the appropriate probability. That is, for the fund decision the options price is given by .75 * $89.09K + .25 * $52.72K = $80K. This options price can be the input, instead of gain, that serves as the objective function for the integer programming application. A similar computation for project B gives Table 11.3, showing the outcomes and their NPV. The probability is computed as 0.5 and hence the final value is 0.5 * $77.27K + 0.50 * $48.18 = $62.72K. Notice that this is lower than the value for project B and that this will probably lead to a different portfolio than in previous attempts.

The options value can be used in several ways to now select the project portfolio. This number is the amount that one should be willing to pay at the feasibility phase in order to avoid the potential reduced project value one year later. One could argue that the best projects are those that have the highest values regardless of the actual expected value of the project. Figure 11.1 shows the code for this integer problem and Figure 11.2 shows the output.

Notice that in this case the optimal profile based on these options prices is the same as that selected using the original gains.

Table 11.3 The simple options example with options pricing.

Branch	Cost step 1	Value at step 2	Value–cost at step 2	NPV
Fund—increase	$10K	$96K	$86K	$77.27K
Fund—decrease	$10K	$64K	$54K	$48.18K
Do not fund	$0K	$0K	$0K	$0 K

```
data simple;
input _id_ $ p1 p2 _type_ $ _rhs_;
cards;
options 80 62.72 max .
cost 20 10 1e 15
available 1 1 upperbd .
available 0 0 lowerbd .
integer 1 1 integer .
;
proc lp data=simple; run;
```

Figure 11.1 Code for the simple options price–based portfolio selection.

```
                    Variable Summary
        Variable                                        Reduced
  Col  Name     Status  Type       Price  Activity       Cost
    1  p1               BINARY       80       0           80
    2  p2               BINARY      62.72     1          62.72
    3  cost     BASIC   SLACK        0        5           0
                   Constraint Summary
        Constraint        S/S                           Dual
  Row  Name     Type      Col      Rhs   Activity     Activity
    1  options  OBJECTVE   .        0     62.72          .
    2  cost     LE         3       15      10
```

Figure 11.2 Output for the simple options price–based portfolio selection.

OPTIONS PRICING APPROACH APPLIED TO A REALISTIC PORTFOLIO PROBLEM

As a more realistic example of this real options approach, consider the 20-project portfolio selection process that has been introduced in previous chapters. Remember that there are various constraints on the training, business objectives, and total risk that are still in effect even if one uses the options price instead of gain. The simple approach to this problem is to compute the options pricing values for each project separately and then maximize this with the integer program.

Here are the details for working out the options pricing for the first project on the list. Table 11.4 provides a review of the potential 20-project list.

For each project, including project 1, there are the same three options that were present in the simple example: fund with an increase, fund with a decrease, and do not fund. If it is assumed that the interest rate is 10 percent and that each project will take one year to mature, and that the up and down movements are always 20 percent, then the computation goes as follows. Table 11.5 shows the NPV computations for this project.

Table 11.4 The 20-project Six Sigma example data.

Project name	Gain $100K	Cost $100K	% failure	Directive	Training
Project A	2	0.3	25	1	GB
Project C	10	0.3	12	2	GB
Project D	8	0.2	5	2, 3	BB
Project E	25	5.0	50	1, 2, 3	MBB
Project F	5	1.0	5	3	BB
Project G	5	0.8	10	3	GB
Project H	7	0.2	25	2	BB
Project J	11	0.7	35	1	GB
Project K	4	1.0	25	1	GB
Project L	50	4.0	35	3	MBB
Project M	16	8.0	40	1, 2	BB
Project N	26	1.2	70	1, 3	MBB
Project P	1	0.2	70	3	GB
Project Q	3	0.3	37	1	BB
Project R	8	0.8	25	1	BB
Project S	5	0.8	12	2	GB
Project T	5	1.8	3	1	GB
Project U	22	10.0	18	2, 3	BB
Project V	38	10.0	80	1, 2, 3	MBB
Project W	9	0.9	40	1, 3	BB

Table 11.5 The NPV values that apply to each of the 20 projects.

Branch	Cost step 1	Value at step 2	Value–cost at step 2	NPV
Fund—increase	$30K	$240K	$210K	$188.18K
Fund—decrease	$30K	$160K	$130K	$115.45K
Do not fund	$0K	$0K	$0K	$0 K

Table 11.6 The options values for the 20 projects.

Project name	Gain $100K	Cost $100K	Probability	Options value
Project A	2	0.3	0.75	1.7
Project C	10	0.3	0.75	9.7
Project D	8	0.2	0.75	7.8
Project E	25	5.0	0.75	20.0
Project F	5	1.0	0.75	4.0
Project G	5	0.8	0.75	4.2
Project H	7	0.2	0.75	6.8
Project J	11	0.7	0.75	10.3
Project K	4	1.0	0.75	2.97
Project L	50	4.0	0.75	46.0
Project M	16	8.0	0.75	8.0
Project N	26	1.2	0.75	24.8
Project P	1	0.2	0.75	0.8
Project Q	3	0.3	0.75	2.7
Project R	8	0.8	0.75	7.2
Project S	5	0.8	0.75	4.2
Project T	5	1.8	0.75	3.2
Project U	22	10.0	0.75	12.0
Project V	38	10.0	0.75	28.0
Project W	9	0.9	0.75	8.10

The probability of increase is given by p ($240K) + $(1-p)$ ($160K) = 1.1 * $200K, which allows one to solve for $p = 0.75$. Then the options value for project 1 is computed as 0.75 * $188.18K + 0.25 * $115.45K = $170K. Continuing in this manner for the other 19 projects gives the options values shown in Table 11.6.

The code to maximize this options value is shown in Figure 11.3 and the output in Figure 11.4. This project portfolio consists of projects 3, 5 through 8, 10, 12, 15, 16, 18, and 19 while the integer solution for maximizing gain given in Chapter 6 was 2 through 5, 10, and 15 through 19, so these two solutions are different to some extent.

Options Pricing Approaches to Six Sigma Project Portfolio Selection 143

```
data c822examp;
input _id_ $ p1-p20 _type_ $ _rhs_;
cards;
options 1.7 9.7 7.8 20 4 4.2 6.8 10.3 2.97 46 8 24.8 0.8 2.7 7.2
4.2 3.2 12 28 8.1 max .
gain 2 8.5 8.2 20 5 5 7 11 4 30 16 26 1 3 10 4.5 5 25 36 9 max .
cost .3 .4 .3 4.5 1 .8 .2 .7     1 5 8 1.2 .2 .3 2 .5 1.5 12 15
.9 le 40
risk 25 100 0 100 0 10 25 35      25      100 40 70 70 37 0 0 0
0 0 40 le 250
direct1 1 0 0 1 0 0 0 1 1 0 1  1  0 1 1 0 1 0 1 1 ge 3
direct2 0 2 2 0 0 0 2 0 0 0 0  0  0 0 2 0 2 0 0 ge 3
direct3 0 0 0 0 3 3 0 0 0 3 0  0  3 0 0 0 0 0 0 0 ge 3
train1  1 1 0 0 0 1 0 1 1 0 0  0  1 0 0 1 1 0 0 1 ge 3
train2  0 0 2 0 2 0 2 0 0 0 2  0  0 2 2 0 0 2 0 0 ge 3
train3  0 0 0 3 0 0 0 0 0 3 0  3  0 0 0 0 0 3 0 ge 3
available 1 1 1 1 1 1 1 1 1 1 1 1 1 1 1 1 1 1 1 1 upperbd .
available 0 0 0 0 0 0 0 0 0 0 0 0 0 0 0 0 0 0 0 0 lowerbd .
integer 1 1 1 1 1 1 1 1 1 1 1 1 1 1 1 1 1 1 1 1 integer .
;
title 'c8 ex 2';
proc lp data=c822examp;
run;
```

Figure 11.3 The linear programming code for the 20-project options pricing.

```
                        Variable Summary
        Variable                                    Reduced
Col    Name     Status  Type       Price  Activity  Cost
  1    p1               BINARY      1.7      0       1.7
  2    p2               BINARY      9.7      0       9.7
  3    p3               BINARY      7.8      1       7.8
  4    p4               BINARY     20        0      20
  5    p5               BINARY      4        1       4
  6    p6               BINARY      4.2      1       4.2
  7    p7               BINARY      6.8      1       6.8
  8    p8               BINARY     10.3      1      10.3
  9    p9               BINARY      2.97     0       2.97
 10    p10              BINARY     46        1      46
 11    p11              BINARY      8        0       8
 12    p12              BINARY     24.8      1      24.8
 13    p13              BINARY      0.8      0       0.8
 14    p14              BINARY      2.7      0       2.7
 15    p15              BINARY      7.2      1       7.2
 16    p16              BINARY      4.2      1       4.2
 17    p17              BINARY      3.2      0       3.2
```

Figure 11.4 The linear programming output for the 20-project options pricing.

```
                        Variable Summary
        Variable                                           Reduced
   Col  Name     Status  Type       Price    Activity     Cost

    18  p18              BINARY       12        1           12
    19  p19              BINARY       28        1           28
    20  p20              BINARY        8.1      0            8.1
    21  cost     BASIC   SLACK         0        1.3          0
    22  risk     BASIC   SLACK         0       10            0
    23  direct1  BASIC   SURPLUS       0        1            0
    24  direct2  BASIC   SURPLUS       0        5            0
    25  direct3  BASIC   SURPLUS       0        6            0
    26  train1   DEGEN   SURPLUS       0        0            0
    27  train2   BASIC   SURPLUS       0        7            0
    28  train3   BASIC   SURPLUS       0        6            0

   c11  ex 2
                        The LP Procedure
                        Constraint Summary

        Constraint              S/S                        Dual
   Row  Name     Type           Col     Rhs    Activity    Activity

     1  options  OBJECTVE         .       0     155.3        .
     2  cost     LE              21      40      38.7        0
     3  risk     LE              22     250     240          0
     4  direct1  GE              23       3       4          0
     5  direct2  GE              24       3       8          0
     6  direct3  GE              25       3       9          0
     7  train1   GE              26       3       3          0
     8  train2   GE              27       3      10          0
     9  train3   GE              28       3       9          0
```

Figure 11.4 *Continued.*

OPTIONS PRICING WITH DIFFERENT TRANSITION PROBABILITIES

For these initial examples the probability of an increase in value was chosen so as to be neutral but in real applications this probability may better be chosen by internal considerations. And it may vary from project to project. Table 11.7 shows the 20 projects updated with a new transition probability value for each project that is assigned by a company department. This table also shows the resultant options values under these new assumptions.

Figure 11.5 shows the code for the integer program for this modified portfolio selection problem with Figure 11.6 showing the output. This newest optimal project portfolio consists of projects 3, 5 through 8, 10, 12, 15, 16, 18, and 19.

Table 11.7 The options values with differing probabilities.

Project name	Gain $100K	Cost $100K	Interest %	Options value $100K
Project A	2	0.3	0.75	1.88
Project C	10	0.3	0.50	9.65
Project D	8	0.2	0.50	7.76
Project E	25	5.0	0.10	15.98
Project F	5	1.0	0.50	3.98
Project G	5	0.8	0.50	4.18
Project H	7	0.2	0.50	6.77
Project J	11	0.7	0.10	8.53
Project K	4	1.0	0.50	2.98
Project L	50	4.0	0.50	45.5
Project M	16	8.0	0.75	9.47
Project N	26	1.2	0.10	20.62
Project P	1	0.2	0.10	0.64
Project Q	3	0.3	0.10	2.22
Project R	8	0.8	0.75	7.93
Project S	5	0.8	0.50	4.18
Project T	5	1.8	0.50	3.18
Project U	22	10.0	0.50	11.89
Project V	38	10.0	0.10	21.89
Project W	9	0.9	0.50	8.06

```
data c11bexamp;
input _id_ $ p1-p20 _type_ $ _rhs_;
cards;
options 1.88 9.65 7.76 15.98 3.98 4.18 6.77 8.53 2.98 45.75 9.47
20.62 0.64 2.22 7.93 4.18 3.18 11.89 21.89 8.06 max .
cost .3 .4 .3 4.5 1 .8 .2 .7 1 5 8 1.2 .2 .3 2 .5 1.5 12 15 .9 le
40
risk 25 100 0 100 0 10 25 35 25 100 40 70 70 37 0 0 0 0 0 40 le
250
direct1 1 0 0 1 0 0 0 1 1 0 1 1 0 1 1 0 1 0 1 1 ge 3
direct2 0 2 2 0 0 0 2 0 0 0 0 0 0 0 2 0 2 0 0 ge 3
```

Figure 11.5 The linear programming code for differing probabilities.

```
direct3    0 0 0 0 3 3 0 0 0 3 0 0 3 0 0 0 0 0 0 0 ge 3
train1     1 1 0 0 0 1 0 1 1 0 0 0 1 0 0 1 1 0 0 1 ge 3
train2     0 0 2 0 2 0 2 0 0 0 2 0 0 2 2 0 0 2 0 0 ge 3
train3     0 0 0 3 0 0 0 0 0 3 0 3 0 0 0 0 0 0 3 0 ge 3
available  1 1 1 1 1 1 1 1 1 1 1 1 1 1 1 1 1 1 1 1 upperbd .
available  0 0 0 0 0 0 0 0 0 0 0 0 0 0 0 0 0 0 0 0 lowerbd .
integer    1 1 1 1 1 1 1 1 1 1 1 1 1 1 1 1 1 1 1 1 integer .
;
title 'c11 ex 3';
proc lp data=c11bexamp;
run;
```

Figure 11.5 *Continued.*

			Variable Summary			
	Variable					Reduced
Col	Name	Status	Type	Price	Activity	Cost
1	p1		BINARY	1.88	0	1.88
2	p2		BINARY	9.65	0	9.65
3	p3		BINARY	7.76	1	7.76
4	p4		BINARY	15.98	0	15.98
5	p5		BINARY	3.98	1	3.98
6	p6		BINARY	4.18	1	4.18
7	p7		BINARY	6.77	1	6.77
8	p8		BINARY	8.53	1	8.53
9	p9		BINARY	2.98	0	2.98
10	p10		BINARY	45.75	1	45.75
11	p11		BINARY	9.47	0	9.47
12	p12		BINARY	20.62	1	20.62
13	p13		BINARY	0.64	0	0.64
14	p14		BINARY	2.22	0	2.22
15	p15		BINARY	7.93	1	7.93
16	p16		BINARY	4.18	1	4.18
17	p17		BINARY	3.18	0	3.18
18	p18		BINARY	11.89	1	11.89
19	p19		BINARY	21.89	1	21.89
20	p20		BINARY	8.06	0	8.06
21	cost	BASIC	SLACK	0	1.3	0
22	risk	BASIC	SLACK	0	10	0
23	direct1	BASIC	SURPLUS	0	1	0
24	direct2	BASIC	SURPLUS	0	5	0
25	direct3	BASIC	SURPLUS	0	6	0
26	train1	DEGEN	SURPLUS	0	0	0
27	train2	BASIC	SURPLUS	0	7	0
28	train3	BASIC	SURPLUS	0	6	0

Figure 11.6 The linear programming output for differing probabilities.

```
                    The LP Procedure
                   Constraint Summary
         Constraint           S/S                        Dual
   Row   Name       Type      Col      Rhs   Activity   Activity
     1   options    OBJECTVE    .        0    143.48       .
     2   cost       LE         21       40     38.7        0
     3   risk       LE         22      250    240          0
     4   direct1    GE         23        3      4          0
     5   direct2    GE         24        3      8          0
     6   direct3    GE         25        3      9          0
     7   train1     GE         26        3      3          0
     8   train2     GE         27        3     10          0
     9   train3     GE         28        3      9          0
```

Figure 11.6 *Continued.*

OPTIONS ON PROJECT PORTFOLIOS

It is also possible to compute options values for entire portfolios in a similar way as was accomplished for individual projects. A particular project portfolio, assuming it has a total cost that falls below the budget cap, will have a total cost and total benefit that can be attached to it. Then the NPV can be computed for the entire portfolio and consequently the options value can also be constructed. This is easiest to perform if the transition probabilities do not change with the various projects.

DECISION ANALYSIS AND SIMULATION METHODS

Financial options require the specification of gains, interest rates, and transition probabilities that are in line with openly traded securities and hence are more generic than in their application to project portfolio selection. Often, closed-form solutions can be written for the strictly financial applications. However, for project portfolios it is possible and advantageous to construct decision trees that incorporate the various details of the project reviews. As long as one includes the financial alternative of shuttling the funds from the project to an alternative risk-free investment then one will be calculating something akin to the options value. If this tree is complicated then often a simulation must be used to generate the various possible gains at each step. The tree also allows one to compute an optimal decision strategy, which is usually not a concern in the strict financial options approach (Grant et al. 1997).

It is also feasible to expand the different possibilities at each step from just the two that have been used in the examples in this chapter. In place of the simple 'fund or do not fund' choice there might be ways to change the attributes of the project or assign different management regimes to the projects. There is also the possibility to delay the project rather than simply cancel it. All of these kinds of alternatives can be handled in the options approach. There are general trends that can be surmised about the impacts of different sources of uncertainty including financial, management, and technical risk on the options value (Huchzermeier and Loch 2001).

RISK MITIGATION APPROACHES

One of the more interesting extensions of the real options approach to Six Sigma project portfolio selection revolves around the concept of the sure market investment that is often used in the financial options arena. In the financial world it is assumed that it is always possible to invest the money that would have gone into a riskier instrument into an investment with a fixed but guaranteed return. This assumption means that it is always possible to extract a gain with little or no risk but that this investment might be outperformed by another riskier investment. The options price is one way of measuring the difference in these two investments.

In project management it is harder to satisfy this assumption of a sure gain without risk. This means that one might have to do the comparisons between projects that both have risk with one being simply relatively safer than the other. Something like an options price still would seem to be a valid way in which to measure this relative gain, however. Or perhaps there should not be a single low-risk project that is used for this purpose but a combination of projects similar to the data envelope or efficient horizon–derived project. This kind of flexible baseline investment should mean that projects would have potentially different evaluations based on the set of projects that are up for consideration. It also would seem to indicate that even better performance could be achieved for Six Sigma project portfolios that are constructed in this manner.

RECIPE FOR THE METHOD USED IN THIS CHAPTER

Options Pricing Method

Step 1 Set sequential decision points

Step 2 Choose discount interest rate

Step 3 Choose transition probabilities

Step 4 Compute net present values

Step 5 Compute options values

Step 6 Use these values in a mathematical programming routine

12
Summary and Outlook for Six Sigma Project Portfolio Selection

SIX SIGMA AND PROJECT SELECTION

This book has an ambitious agenda and to accomplish it there has been, by necessity, a great deal of material covered in just a few pages, so it might be advisable to recap the material before considering the future of Six Sigma project portfolio selection. The overarching objective of the book is to demonstrate, firstly, that a project portfolio approach has advantages over a project-by-project selection method and, secondly, that there are many excellent methods that can be easily borrowed from the operations research literature to create such portfolios. Chapter 1 tries to summarize the features that make Six Sigma one of the most popular and successful process improvement approaches ever to be implemented. Although there are many different flavors and brands of Six Sigma, the majority of such programs have been able to produce success by creating a statistically adept workforce, by embedding the program in the real needs of the organization, and by organizing work into right-sized projects that have the appropriate level of support and backing. Although all three of these elements are important and may be worthy of entire books in their own rights, this book concentrates on the Six Sigma project selection process.

Chapter 2 attempts to summarize the project selection method that is typically advocated and applied in Six Sigma programs. Six Sigma projects often have multiple objectives to achieve including those of providing appropriate training, of providing leadership experience, of improving customer satisfaction, of satisfying organizational politics and, most importantly, creating verifiable monetary gains. Depending on the type of organization that is implementing the Six Sigma projects and the maturity of the program, any one of these multiple objectives can come to dominate the others. This book strongly argues that it is the fiscal value that is generated by the project that should be paramount and that all other objectives should best be treated as constraints or as secondary objectives. Based on this assumption it is straightforward to show that a project-by-project selection approach will often be substantially outperformed by an integrated portfolio approach. There are many useful tools that come from well-developed fields of study like operations research and financial engineering that can be readily adopted to enable the selection of high-performance Six Sigma project portfolios.

RANKING METHODS AND MULTIPLE OBJECTIVES

The current methods for Six Sigma project selection use ranking based on each project separately. The characteristics that are often considered desirable for a good Six Sigma project include high benefit, reasonable cost, high customer service value, training value, cross-divisional scope, and manageable risk. In many Six Sigma programs the projects are screened and rated on the basis of characteristics like these. A group of managers then tries to fit the rated potential projects within the budget cap and into the improvement plan, if it exists. Since most companies do not allocate sufficient budget to do all of the proposed projects, the selection process is usually a mixture of ad hoc hurdles that a project must meet and the rest is handled through typically subjective organizational politics. One can argue that subjective input is potentially beneficial in small amounts but it usually does not produce a project portfolio that is nearly as efficient as one created by scientific means. This is primarily due to the fact that the decision makers can modify the method for combining the projects on the spot with respect to their own needs and desires. An integrated portfolio tends to choose the best mix of projects from a more integrated companywide approach.

One improved method that builds upon the standard ranking approach is the *analytical hierarchy process* (AHP). This method begins with a ranking of all the potential projects in a pair-wise fashion for each and every one of the multiple objectives. Another ranking of the objectives themselves is done and produces a set of weights to be used in the combining process. Managers have free reign in creating the relative rankings but do not directly affect the method that is used to unite the disparate projects into one portfolio. This approach can be quite effective for small project portfolio selections but can be difficult to apply to problems with large numbers of projects or with very many project characteristics.

Summary and Outlook for Six Sigma Project Portfolio Selection 153

Another not too dissimilar method is the *multiple criteria decision making* (MCDM) approach. This again uses ranking of the individual projects but in this case the weights are direct inputs from the selection team. This approach can be quite effective if the decision makers are not overtly hostile to each other or to the purposes of the Six Sigma program. Its primary weakness is the fact that the chosen weights are more or less arbitrary but are critical to the creation of the portfolio.

Another ranking-like method for Six Sigma project selection that can outperform the standard methods is *data envelope analysis* (DEA). The DEA method uses characteristics like gain, cost, risk, training value, and business directive coverage of the projects that are given as part of the proposal to construct a reference envelope or horizon for the entire set of projects. This envelope can then be used to establish an optimal project against which the real project may be compared. The distance between this optimal project and the proposed project can provide a ranking of the projects that can then be organized into a portfolio by any of the other methods like AHP or MCDM. Because this method systematically creates the rankings based on the project characteristics themselves, DEA is not subject to the subjective suboptimization that can be an outcome of the standard approach.

LINEAR AND INTEGER PROGRAMMING METHODS

Linear programming is promoted in this book as one of the chief ways in which one can make major improvements in the Six Sigma project portfolio selection process. It does require one to concentrate on gain as the most important objective and to treat other characteristics as elements of various constraints that must be respected in any attempt to optimize the gain. These methods have been used for many decades now and can be shown to provide excellent, quick, precise solutions for the selection of portfolios. If partial investments in projects are possible, then linear programming is the proper choice. Solutions produced by linear programming have a mathematical guarantee that they are the optimal portfolios that can be constructed given the constraints. If the funding must be all or none for each project, then a modification of linear programming called integer programming should be used. For most realistically-sized Six Sigma project portfolios it will take very little execution time or computer resources to compute either the linear or the integer programming solutions.

An important feature that is more or less embedded into linear programming is the sensitivity analysis study. Sensitivity analysis shows how much and in what ways the best portfolio will change if some of the input data or assumptions are changed. For example, the cost estimates may be underestimated by 10 percent consistently by a certain project manager. If this is taken into account then the linear programming methods may produce an entirely different portfolio. Sensitivity analysis can account for this kind of impact. Or if some projects fail unexpectedly then the expected returns will be impaired but the size and direction of the impact on the whole portfolio may be difficult to guess. Again, sensitivity analysis can provide an easy answer to this second type of problem as well. Sensitivity analysis works differently for integer and other forms of programming but it can still be an integral part of the selection procedure.

Two particular types of programming problems that arise quite frequently in Six Sigma project portfolio selection applications are the multidivisional and multiperiod problems. Multiple periods allow one to set the project plan in an optimal fashion across time periods or funding periods. Multidivisional problems allow one to make project portfolios that work well across the different administrative or business groups in an organization. One can also treat both of these issues together in one multiperiod, multidivisional problem. Linear and integer programming can easily be extended to cover these more complex types of project portfolio problems.

NONLINEAR PROGRAMMING AND OPTIONS METHODS

Sometimes the Six Sigma project portfolio selection problem does not fit nicely into the assumptions of linearity that are required to correctly apply the linear and integer programming methods and there might be a need to incorporate nonlinear objectives or constraints. The methods of nonlinear programming can be used in these circumstances to choose a high-performance project portfolio. There are many different approaches to nonlinear programming that can be adapted to the specific details of a problem but often a generic procedure will work well without much tailoring. One common generic procedure of nonlinear programming uses a steepest-descent search from an initial portfolio to achieve better and better final portfolios until no further improvements can be made. Although nonlinear programming methods can sometimes miss the absolute best portfolio they will usually perform well and one should expect them to greatly outdistance the portfolios chosen without their assistance when the problems are nonlinear in nature.

A method that is very popular in the financial engineering or mathematical finance field is the use of an option. An option is an approach that allows the manager to control the risk of a downside effect due to an unexpected subperformance of a project. The correct options price reflects the additional cost that must be incurred at time t_1 to avoid this possible loss at a later time t_2. In this book these options prices are used as a natural way by which to rank projects that can then be assigned to a portfolio by other methods like integer programming. Chapter 11 shows some elementary methods that can be used to properly price the project as an option.

SOME GUIDELINES FOR THE USE OF THE METHODS

Because there are so many different procedures that can be utilized in an attempt to improve the Six Sigma project selection process it may be valuable to discuss the various advantages and disadvantages of each method and to provide some guidance as to their best implementation. It is hoped that this will enable the reader to pick and choose the most suitable method for the unique situation in which they find themselves.

There are four split-points that can be used to classify the different methods in a manner that will guide their implementation. The first dichotomy is that between those methods that treat the multiple characteristics as objectives versus constraints. The standard ranking method, the MCDM methods, the AHP method, and the DEA method all fall on the multiple objective side of this bifurcation. The programming methods, whether they be linear, integer, or nonlinear, belong to the constraint side of the split. The options methods could probably fall on either side of the split but, in this book, the type of applications demonstrated put it in the constraint side since the options price is most often used subsequently in mathematical programming applications. Figure 12.1 illustrates this primary split in the methods.

Now one can consider further splits of each of these two subcategories. Firstly, the "multiple objectives" subcategory can be split further into those methods that require assigned weights and those that construct weights. The assigned-weight methods are ranking and the assigned-weight MCDM while the constructed-weight methods consist of the Pareto, the analytic hierarchy, and the data envelope approaches. This secondary split is illustrated in Figure 12.2.

Finally, the assigned-weight methods can be split between the ranking methods, which use a primarily subjective method, and the assigned-weight method MCDM, which uses an objective method to combine across the objectives. In the constructed-weight subcategory one can separate the analytic hierarchy method, which uses pair-wise rankings to manufacture

156 Chapter Twelve

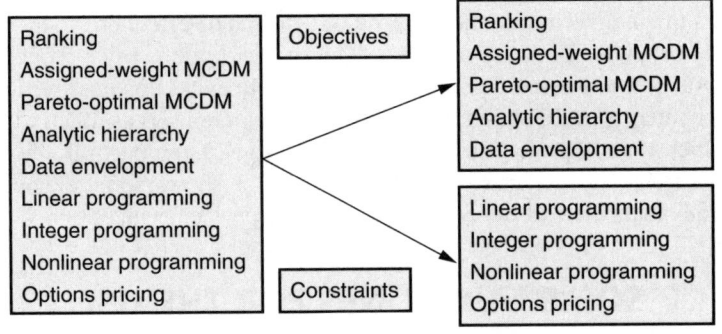

Figure 12.1 The split in methods due to objectives versus constraints.

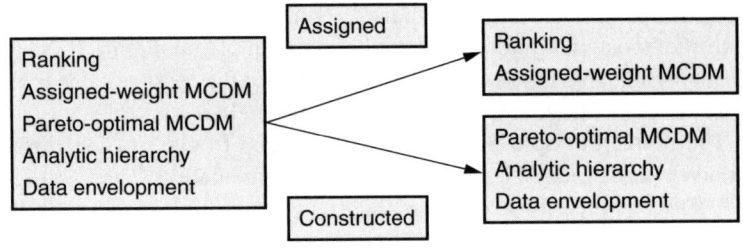

Figure 12.2 The secondary split in the multiple objective subcategory.

the weights, from the Pareto-optimal and data envelopment methods, which use relative project characteristics.

Returning to the original subcategory that was defined by it, consideration of multiple characteristics as one primary objective with constraints, a split can be made between the mathematical programming methods and the financial planning options methods first, then a split of the programming methods between those that guarantee optimal portfolios and those that do not. Specifically, the linear and integer programming methods provide this guarantee while the nonlinear methods do not. All of these divisions are presented in Figure 12.3.

In all cases and for all methods the requirements for application are pretty equivalent in that one needs a list of projects, each with associated attributes like cost, benefit, training value, customer requirements, and strategic business needs. For the multiple objective method one must be able to provide an ordering of the objectives or at least a relative rating in addition to these basic requirements. For the constraint methods one

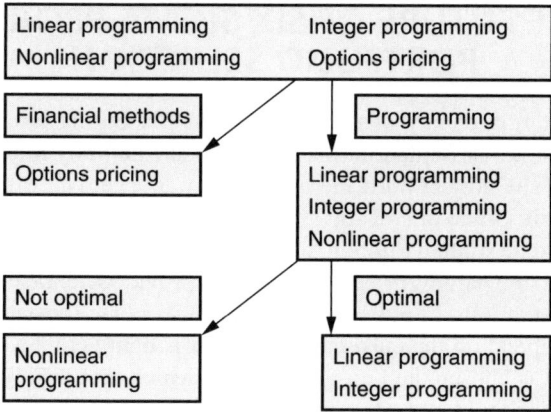

Figure 12.3 The subsequent splits of the constraint subcategory.

must choose a single objective and be able to formulate other needs as constrains. If the objective and constraints are linear then linear programming can be performed; if some constraints require integer values then integer programming is the right choice; and if nonlinearity is required then nonlinear programming is on track. For options pricing one must specify the sequence of decisions, a baseline interest rate, and at least two possible outcomes that are usually a greater and lesser gain for each project.

It is also true that for efficient application the mathematical programming methods require the most sophistication while most of the other methods can be done by hand or by spreadsheet computations. Of course even for these cases it may be far more efficient to create code or macros for the purpose if there are many projects, many characteristics, or if the procedure is to be recomputed often.

Another distinguishing feature that can be used to gauge the right method to try in one's Six Sigma project portfolio selection is the difficulty imposed by very large sets of possible projects with or without lots of complicated secondary objectives. Most of the MCDM methods require that some kind of weighting be given for each project at least and, for some, each pair of projects. In most business situations if would be surprising if more than say 40 projects could be considered in this way if the management team must provide the resources to do the assignment. Even if the mechanism of the procedure can be accomplished for these large and complex situations it can be argued that the results are not likely to be very consistent. In these cases there are definite advantages to the mathematical programming methods although clearly they will also be more complicated to apply as problems become inordinately large.

THE FUTURE OF SIX SIGMA PROJECT PORTFOLIO SELECTION

The implantation of any of the methods for Six Sigma project portfolio selection that are presented in this book can substantially improve the performance of the project portfolio and, more importantly, of the Six Sigma program itself. Since one of the assumptions of Six Sigma is that all processes should be studied through Six Sigma methodology, these approaches fit nicely into the paradigm as these methods provide scientific, quantitative ways to substantially improve performance. Of course the actual improvement will depend on the current method that is being employed, on which new method is chosen, and on the extent to which that deployment is successful, but it should be quite common to get at least a 10 percent improvement in returns. For many Six Sigma programs this could easily mean millions of dollars in additional gains and reduced times to achieve results. If one's current methods are weak or if the selection committee is suspect then one should have a good chance of obtaining even larger gains, perhaps on the order of 25 to 50 percent better, which could have an even more fundamental impact on the way the company does business.

The methods presented here are separated into different chapters in order to make their mechanisms clear for the reader, but there is no reason not to combine the methods as one sees fit to achieve even better performance. Hybrid methods often produce better, more robust solutions than more monocultural approaches. For example, one could use data envelopment analysis of option prices to create new characteristics for each project, which can then be plugged into the integer programming method to construct the final funded portfolio. Or one might take the original Six Sigma ranking method and do a sensitivity analysis on it to show how unstable it might be to the uncertainty inherent in some of the inputs.

Each method has an algorithm that is used to implement it. Excellent work is being done on many of these algorithms and tremendous gains in efficiency are being made continually. Linear programming algorithms are improving in efficiency at a rate much faster than that of the computing machinery on which they run. They are beating Moore's Law by a large degree. In addition, there are improvements in data handling, data preprocessing, and data post-processing that take much of the drudge work out of the hands of the user. Problems that seemed impossible even five years ago because of their sizes are being solved in mere minutes of computation time today.

Six Sigma will advance in new ways once it realizes that its own techniques can be used to guide its development. Two big fields with lots and lots of powerful tools and insights that are not being tapped today are operations research and control engineering. The introduction of project portfolio methods like those presented here should entice Six Sigma practitioners to peek beyond the boundaries of their own world and learn by observing those other fields. It is very likely (think hybrid again!) that these pioneering Six Sigma practitioners will have a dramatically positive impact on Six Sigma even to the point of accelerating its progress by an order of magnitude.

Six Sigma, as powerful and widespread as it is, is just the tip of the iceberg of what process improvement could likely become in the future. Instead of concentrating primarily on manufacturing and R&D, these methods could allow easy access to new applications fields such as administrative processes, decision processes, information processes, and knowledge processes. Most organizations are only dabbling in the middle of a business cycle model that starts with data, leads to information, turns into insight, creates knowledge, and results in actions. Whereas information technology is just beginning to affect the data-to-information step, it is in the insight and knowledge steps that Six Sigma analysis could lead the way. And the way it could get there, to the directors and boards of the company, is through properly chosen and executed project portfolios using methods such as those explained in this book.

Bibliography

Belton, Valerie. 2001. *Multiple Criteria Decision Analysis: An Integrated Approach.* Dordrecht, The Netherlands: Kluwer Academic.

Bowman, Edward H., and Gary T. Moskowitz. 2001. "Real Options Analysis and Strategic Decision Making." *Organization Science* 12, no. 6 (Nov.–Dec.): 772–77.

Brassard, Michael, and Diane Ritter. 2001. *Sailing Through Six Sigma.* Marietta, GA: Brassard & Ritter.

Broadie, Mark, and Jerome B. Detemple. 2004. "Option Pricing: Valuation Models and Applications." *Management Science* 50, no. 9 (Sept.): 1145–77.

George, Michael L. 2002. *Lean Six Sigma.* New York: McGraw-Hill.

Grant, Dwight, Gautam Vora, and David Weeks. 1997. "Path-Dependent Options: Extending the Monte Carlo Simulation Approach." *Management Science* 43, no. 11 (Nov.): 1589–1602.

Harry, Mikel J. *Six Sigma Story* Web site (2006). http://www.mikeljharry.com/story.php.

Hillier, Frederick S., and Gerald J. Lieberman. 1974. *Operations Research,* 2nd ed. San Francisco: Holden-Day.

Huchzermeier, Arnd, and Christoph H. Loch. 2001. "Project Management Under Risk: Using the Real Options Approach to Evaluate Flexibility in R&D." *Management Science* 47, no. 1 (Jan.): 85–101.

Mawby, William D. 2005. *Decision Process Quality Management.* Milwaukee: ASQ Quality Press.

Raphael, Benny, and Ian F. C. Smith. 2003. *Fundamentals of Computer-Aided Engineering.* New York: John Wiley & Sons.

Saaty, Thomas L. 1980. *The Analytic Hierarchy Process.* New York: McGraw Hill.

SAS Institute. 1989. *SAS/OR User's Guide, Version 6,* 1st ed. Cary, NC: SAS Institute.

———. 1994. *Market Analysis Using the SAS System*. Cary, NC: SAS Institute.

———. 1997. *SAS/OR Technical Report: The NLP Procedure*. Cary, NC: SAS Institute.

Six Sigma Web site. 2006. http://www.isixsigma.com.co.six_sigma.

Smith, James E., and Robert F. Nau. 1995. "Valuing Risky Projects: Options Pricing Theory and Decision Analysis." *Management Science* 41, no. 5 (May): 795–816.

Westcott, Russell T. 2004. *Simplified Project Management for the Quality Professional*. Milwaukee: ASQ Quality Press.

Wikipedia Internet Encyclopedia. 2006. "Six Sigma." en.wikipedia.org/wiki/Six_sigma.

Index

A

analytic hierarchy process (AHP),
    37–45, 152
  example, 39–42
  problems with, 44–45
  procedure, 38–39
  with project portfolios, 42–44
  recipe, 45
assigned-weight MCDM method,
    28–30
  problem with, 37–38

B

baseline project, 47–48
branch-and-bound approach, to
    integer programming, 76–78
business plan, in Six Sigma project
    selection, 7

C

classification, of project portfolio
    selection methods, 155–56
constrained portfolios, versus
    unconstrained, 97
constraints
  additional, in integer
      programming, 81–82
  in linear programming, 64–65
  nonlinear, 129
  versus objectives, 61–62

D

data, supporting, 16
data envelopment analysis (DEA),
    47–59, 153
  of entire portfolios, 55–59
  example (complex), 55
  example (simple), 49–54
  recipe, 59
decision analysis, in options pricing
    approach to project portfolio
    selection, 147–48
define–measure–analyze–improve–
    control (DMAIC) cycle, 9
dominated project portfolios, 32–35
dynamic allocation, 135–36

E

employees, use of statistical methods
    by, 5

F

financial accountability/impact, of
 Six Sigma projects, 4–5, 15–16
 in project selection, 13–14

G

General Electric Company, 1–2

H

horizon, in data envelopment analysis, 47–49

I

integer programming, in project portfolio selection, 75–91, 153–54
 additional constraints, 81–82
 in multidivisional approach, 114–16
 in multiperiod approach, 107
 need for, 75–78
 realistic example, 79–81
 recipe, 91
 sensitivity analysis for, 85–91

L

lean manufacturing, 3
Lean Six Sigma, 2–3
linear programming, 153–54
 application to project portfolio selection, 63–70
 recipe, 73
 weakness of, 75

M

managers, versus quality professionals, 6–7

mathematical programming, for project portfolio selection, 61–73, 157
 advantages of, 62
 constraints versus objectives, 61–62
 in multidivisional approach, 114–16
 in multiperiod approach, 107
Motorola, Inc., 1
multidivisional approach, to project portfolio selection, 105, 114–20, 154
multiperiod approaches, to project portfolio selection, 105–7, 119–20, 154
multiple criteria
 conversion to common criterion, 26–28
 need for, 25
multiple criteria decision making (MCDM) methods, 153
 assigned-weight method, 28–30
 Pareto-optimal method, 30–35, 36
 recipe, 35
 for Six Sigma project selection, 25–35

N

net present value (NPV), 138
nonlinear programming, for project portfolio selection, 121–33, 154
 addition of a nonlinear constraint, 129
 example (complex), 124–26
 example (simple), 123–24
 need for nonlinear models, 121–23
 nonlinear sensitivity analysis, 131–33
 recipe, 133

O

objectives, versus constraints, 61–62

options
  definition, 136–37
  on project portfolios, 147
options pricing approaches, to project portfolio selection, 135–49, 154–55
  decision analysis and simulation methods, 147–48
  example (complex), 140–42
  example (simple), 137–39
  need for dynamic allocation, 135–36
  options on project portfolios, 147
  options pricing with different transition probabilities, 144
  recipe, 149
  risk mitigation approaches, 148
  what options are, 136–37

P

Pareto-optimal MCDM method, 30–35
  versus data envelopment analysis, 47
process indicators, in project tracking, 14–15
project evaluation, and project portfolio performance measurement, 96–97
project portfolio
  advantages of constructing, 18–21
  analytic hierarchy process with, 42–44
  dominated, 32–35
  with risk constraints, 21–24
project portfolio performance, analysis
  full sensitivity-based, 101–3
  and sensitivity analysis, 95
project portfolio performance, definition, 93–95
project portfolio performance, measuring, 93–103
  example (simple), 95–97
  gain distribution approach, 97–98
  other approaches, 103
  sensitivity analysis in, 98–99
project portfolio selection
  application of linear programming to, 63–70
  future of, 158–59
  through integer programming, 75–91
  through mathematical programming, 61–73
  multidivisional approaches, 105, 114–20
  multiperiod approaches, 105–7, 119–20
  nonlinear programming for, 121–33
  options pricing approaches, 135–49
  outlook, 151–59
  summary, 151–59
    guidelines, 155–57
project portfolio selection methods, classification, 155–56
project selection
  considerations, 12–13
  typical methods, 10–12
projects, Six Sigma. *See* Six Sigma projects
projects, structured, 4, 5–6

Q

quality professionals, versus managers, 6–7

R

ranking methods, of project selection, 152
  weakness of, 12
risk constraints, portfolios with, 21–24
risk mitigation, in options pricing approach to project portfolio selection, 148

S

SAS linear programming software, 49–50
SAS nonlinear programming procedure code, 122
sensitivity analysis, 62, 71, 153–54
   for integer programming, 85–91
   nonlinear, 131–33
   and project portfolio performance analysis, 95, 101–3
   in project portfolio performance measurement, 98–99
simulation methods, in options approach to project portfolio selection, 147–48
Six Sigma, history, 1–3
Six Sigma program
   elements of successful, 4–5
   structured projects, emphasis on, 5–6
Six Sigma projects
   alignment with business strategy, 15
   characteristics of, 9–24
   emphasis on, 5–6
   the essential, 6–8
   financial accountability/impact of, 4–5, 12–13, 15–16
   identification of, 1–8
   recommendations for, 9–15
   scope of, 16
statistical methods, use of by employees, 5

T

transition probability, 144

U

unconstrained portfolios, versus constrained, 97

V

voice of the customer (VOC), in project selection, 10